BIG
TRAILS

BIG
TRAILS

GREAT BRITAIN & IRELAND

VP

Vertebrate Publishing, Sheffield
www.v-publishing.co.uk

BIG
TRAILS
GREAT BRITAIN
& IRELAND

First published in 2020 by Vertebrate Publishing.

VP **Vertebrate Publishing**
Omega Court, 352 Cemetery Road, Sheffield S11 8FT, United Kingdom.
www.v-publishing.co.uk

ISBN 978-1-83981-000-8 (Paperback)
ISBN 978-1-83981-001-5 (Ebook)

Front cover: Approaching Shiel Bridge on the Cape Wrath Trail. © Sandro Koster
Back cover (left): On Bolberry Down in Devon, overlooking Soar Mill Cove on the South West Coast Path. © Stephen Ross;
(right): Trail running in the Black Mountains on Offa's Dyke. © John Coefield
Individual photography as credited.

Mapping contains Openstreetmap.org data ©OpenStreetMap contributors, CC BY-SA and data licensed from ©EuroGeographics.
Cartography by Richard Ross, **Active Maps Ltd.** – *www.activemaps.co.uk*

Cover design by Jane Beagley, Vertebrate Publishing.
Interior book design by **Ryder Design** – *www.ryderdesign.studio*
Production by Cameron Bonser, Vertebrate Publishing.

Printed and bound in Europe by Latitude Press.

Vertebrate Publishing is committed to printing on paper from sustainable sources.

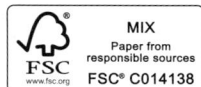

THE CAMBRIAN WAY CLIMBS OVER CRIBYN. ▶
© ADAM LONG

CONTENTS

THE TRAILS

INTRODUCTION

A Big Trail may be the biggest adventure you'll ever have. Paths have always connected us; paths take us to new places and show us the way home. They offer escape, adventure, an unimagined future. On a Big Trail, you will make friends, enjoy amazing panoramas, sit in silence under starry skies, and occasionally feel that reaching the end of the trail is impossible. Everyone has their own reasons for attempting a Big Trail, and everyone's experience on the trail is unique.

The idea for this book came about in the Refuge de Carrozzu, the second refuge on Corsica's GR20. A dozen shattered walkers and runners huddled together; half had decided to abandon the trail. Waiting for the rain to stop, we had plenty of time to talk and it was very clear that most of those on the trail had no realistic view of what they were letting themselves in for and also no perception of the wide range of amazing alternatives that are available throughout Europe. A Big Trail may be the biggest adventure you'll ever have. It may also be the worst trip you've ever taken – if you choose the wrong trail.

We believe that there is a Big Trail for everyone; Europe offers some of the best long-distance routes in the world. There are the iconic trails that we have all heard of, the trails that are mentioned in hallowed tones in every bunkhouse and campsite across Europe. There are also the trails that you've never heard of; the trails that are just as beautiful, just as challenging, just as diverting as the famous ones. This book describes the trails that you've always wanted to know more about, and the ones that you've never heard of before.

We are passionate about Big Trails. We walk and run them; we read about them; we talk to the people who know them best. We decided to research the very best long-distance trails across Europe, and find out all the information that you might want to know before you pick your next Big Trail. This book is packed full of practical information, beautiful photos, useful maps, facts and figures. There are trails in the mountains, trails around cities, trails along the coast, trails to walk in the summer, trails to run on the shortest days of the year. We hope that this book will help you find your next Big Trail. Be careful – you may find yourself yearning to complete them all.

ACKNOWLEDGEMENTS

We are grateful to the following photographers who have generously allowed us to reproduce their stunning images: Thomas & Jon Barton, Tracy Burton, Jen & Sim Benson, Mike Brocklehurst, Gaurav Chandra, Roger Clegg, John Coefield, Will Copestake, Adrian Hendroff, Deirdre Huston, Christine James, Andrew Lewis, Adam Long, Claire Maxted, Hendrik Morkel, Anna Paxton, Mark Rainsley, Alex Roddie, Stephen Ross, George Tod and Paul and Helen Webster. Thanks go to the following organisations who have helped us source the photography and provided information – many are tireless advocates for, and caretakers of, these Big Trails; Cambrian Way Trust (www.cambrianway.org.uk), Contours Holidays (www.contours.co.uk), Dales Way Association (www.dalesway.org), Friends of A Dales High Way (www.daleshighway.co.uk), Friends of the Ridgeway (www.ridgewayfriends.org.uk), Hadrian's Wall Gallery (www.hadrianswallgallery.com), Icknield Way Association (www.icknieldwaypath.co.uk), Outdoorista (www.outdoorista.co.uk), Wild Ginger Running (wildgingerrunning.co.uk).

We are indebted to Kingsley Jones and Stephen Ross for allowing us to reproduce the Jones–Ross formula which has been used to calculate the trail timings in this book. Stephen thanks his father, Peter, and brother, Richard, for sharing his first Big Trail adventure on the West Highland Way. More recently to Amy, Magnus and Oscar for being willing to join in exploring new routes and to Sarah for her support and dot watching over the years. He hopes this book will inspire her to join him in future expeditions.

◀ CROMER RIDGE, THE HIGHEST POINT IN EAST ANGLIA, ON THE NORFOLK COAST PATH. © ANNA PAXTON

WHAT IS A BIG TRAIL?

A Big Trail is an adventure to be had on foot. It is a long-distance trail, suitable for walkers and runners, that requires several days or weeks to complete. This book presents the very best Big Trails in Great Britain and Ireland. The routes we have chosen for the *Big Trails* series are generally between 100 and 1,000 kilometres in length – although there are a few shorter trails that are simply too good not to mention, and some trails that form part of longer European routes. None of these trails require climbing or winter mountain skills (unless tackled out of season) and most are waymarked although you may still need to navigate, particularly in bad weather. Although some of these trails are more challenging than others, most are suitable for any walker or runner, with sufficient preparation, training and planning.

Every Big Trail is a unique adventure. Some climb over mountain ranges, and some follow the path of a river. Some offer sandy beaches, and some chalky ridges.

You might enjoy Britain's freshest seafood, or discover Iron Age forts on high grassy hills. Some traverse from coast-to-coast, some follow ancient borders or historic trading routes, some climb up and down over beautiful sea cliffs.

A Big Trail might reveal the landscape that inspired painters and poets, offer evenings of traditional music and cameradie, or follow in the footsteps of the Celts, Romans, Saxons, Normans, all the other Europeans before you. The mossy, peaty moorlands offer a soft bed on wild paths best completed with a tent on your back. On other trails, Britain and Ireland's traditional pubs wait for you at the end of each day to offer a fireside to dry your boots beside, a hearty meal and a comfy bed. Some of these trails won't appeal to you. They will be too hilly, too flat, too boggy, too urban or just the wrong length. But whether you're a speedy runner, a mountain goat, a keen landscape photographer or a long luncher, this book has Big Trails to delight you.

CAMPING BY LOCH LOMOND ON THE WEST HIGHLAND WAY. © ALEX RODDIE

ABOUT THE ROUTES

Big Trails: Great Britain & Ireland provides descriptions of Big Trails in England, Scotland, Wales, Northern Ireland, Ireland and the Isle of Man. The most westerly route is **the Beara Way**, an undiscovered treasure on Ireland's wild Atlantic coast, and the most easterly is the **Peddars Way and Norfolk Coast Path**, through the flat farmland and along the sandy seaside of gentle Norfolk. The routes stretch from the isolated, unmarked paths of northern Scotland's **Cape Wrath Trail** to the iconic white cliffs of the sunny **South Downs Way**. At nearly 1,000 kilometres, the **South West Coast Path** around the entire tip of south-western England is the longest route featured in this volume. The shortest route – the **Causeway Coast Way** – reveals crumbling castles, quiet beaches and the natural wonder of the world, the Giant's Causeway on Northern Ireland's beautiful coast. The **Cambrian Way** which climbs over every Welsh mountain range is the route with most ascent (approximately 17,000 metres) and the **Thames Path** which follows England's greatest river from its source in the Cotswolds to the great city of London climbs only 1,000 metres in total.

The routes in this book pass through some of Europe's most beautiful national parks and stunning coastlines. The **Pennine Way** travels through the Yorkshire Dales and the Peak District, and the **Dales Way** crosses from the Yorkshire Dales to the Lakes. The **Kerry Way** is on Ireland's wild Atlantic coast, the **Isle of Anglesey Coastal Path** encircles an island at the very edge of the Welsh coast, while the **South West Coast Path** takes in the fossil-rich Jurassic Coast and the palm-lined resorts of the English Riviera.

THE TRAILS AT A GLANCE

- Twenty trails are linear, and five are circular or near circular. Five (**Wainwright's Coast to Coast, Offa's Dyke Path**, the **John Muir Way**, the **Cambrian Way** and **Hadrian's Wall Path**) cross the country from coast to coast.

- Ten routes are National Trails (including the **Cotswold Way** and the **Pennine Way**) and two are Scotland's Great Trails (the **John Muir Trail** and **West Highland Way**).

- Seven trails are coastal but four more combine country with a coastal stretch (the **Cape Wrath Trail**, the **Cleveland Way, Peddars Way and the Norfolk Coast Path** and the **South Downs Way**).

- Four trails (**Wicklow Way, London LOOP, Thames Path** and the **Cambrian Way**) start or end in a country's capital.

- Two trails take historic border defences as their guide (**Offa's Dyke Path** and **Hadrian's Wall Path**) and three (**the Ridgeway, Icknield Way Path** and **Peddars Way**) follow the route of the ancient Greater Ridgeway road across southern England.

OUR FAVOURITES

We think that every single Big Trail in this book is special, and there is something unique about every one of them that has earned them a place in *Big Trails: Great Britain & Ireland*. But if you're not sure what to look at first, here are five of our favourites.

- Thousands walk the **West Highland Way** every year, and you're bound to meet plenty of fellow adventurers on this iconic route as you walk from Scotland's friendliest city to the foot of its biggest mountain through dramatic Highland scenery. If you want to swap tales of the trail in bunkhouses and hostels, or enjoy traditional music and a pint in a country pub, the West Highland Way is Britain's *Friendliest Trail.*

IRELAND'S WILD ATLANTIC COAST ON THE BEARA WAY. © THOMAS BARTON

- Although the remote Cape Wrath Trail and the month-long South West Coast Path are tough contenders, the **Cambrian Way** is our *Wildest Adventure*. It takes you across the Black Mountains, the Brecon Beacons, the Rhinogydd and through Snowdonia over Wales' highest mountain. You'll walk from the Welsh capital into the country's Green Desert and have the opportunity to stay in remote wilderness hostels, and enjoy the Welsh seaside.

- It's up to you whether you run the high moorland paths or the technical ups and downs of the Yorkshire cliffs, or both, but the **Cleveland Way** is *Great for Trail Running*. There's a fresh sea breeze to keep you cool, and you can stop for ice cream in Robin Hood's Bay and fish and chips in Whitby.

- Kerry bustles with tourists, but fewer visit the wild shores of its Atlantic neighbour, Beara. The **Beara Way** winds a green path around Ireland's most western coast, encircling two islands, and passing stone circles, tombs and a cable car above the ocean waves on Ireland's *Best Off the Beaten Track Trail*.

- The **Causeway Coast Way** is a little Big Trail that packs a lot of coast, castles and charm – and even the Giant's Causeway , considered by many to be one of the Natural Wonders of the World – into fifty-three kilometres. It is a *Great Weekend Escape*, easy enough to do in a long weekend and still have the energy for an evening out in Belfast.

- The **Raad ny Foillan** or Way of the Gull encircles the friendly, sunny Isle of Man. This route is *Perfect for All the Family* – there are electric and steam trains, and even horse-drawn trams should you get tired en route. You can discover lighthouses and castles, a giant wheel and a fairy bridge, a wildlife park with a fugitive red panda and Davison's ice cream.

HOW TO USE THIS BOOK

This book provides descriptions of twenty-five of the very best European long-distance trails in England, Scotland, Wales, Northern Ireland, Ireland and the Isle of Man. Each route description provides you with the following information.

- An overview of the route from start to finish.

- Useful information on how to get there, when to go and what to expect.

- Essential information on accommodation, weather and terrain.

- Highlights along the way – historical sites en route, wildlife to look out for, the best views.

- Interesting facts about the places you'll pass.

- A summary of route variations and detours.

This book is not intended to let you plan your next Big Trail adventure, but rather to inspire you. Whether you want a hilly challenge or a seaside amble, solitude or camaraderie, local beer, historic castles or ancient woods, this book has the trail for you. It includes iconic trails, such as **Wainwright's Coast to Coast** and the **West Highland Way**, but also undiscovered gems such as the **Isle of Anglesey Coastal Path**, which encircles the Welsh island, and **A Dales High Way** which takes you on a higher route over the peaceful Yorkshire Dales. Each route description is accompanied by beautiful photography to give you a sense of what to expect on the trail.

The trails are presented in alphabetical order so that you can easily find the one you're interested in. But if you're not sure where to start, why not turn to the back of the book where you'll find our unique trail index that quickly allow you to find a trail based on where it is, how long is it (kilometres or days) or when to go?

In addition to detailed descriptions and inspiring photography, at the end of each trail a handy double page of the following essential information is provided.

- An overview map of the trail, which shows the route (and major variations), terrain, nearby towns and cities, and other local features.

- Trail length, and cumulative ascent and descent.

- An elevation profile of the route.

- Details of the start and finish, and how to get there, including information on the closest international air, rail or ferry connections.

- Days to complete the trail – for Walkers. Trekkers, Fastpackers and Trail runners, calculated using the Jones–Ross formula (information on the Jones–Ross formula and different trail users is prov ded on pages XVII–XVIII).

- Pros and cons to offer a quick insight into the trail.

- Information about the most common accommodation options available on or close to the trai .

- Details about trail characteristics and the paths that you will encounter on the trail.

- An indication of waymarking on the trail.

- A calendar showing months when the trail can be safely completed.

- How to find further information – details of Vertebrate Publishing's guidebooks and guidemaps, trail websites and other guidebooks or maps that will provide more detailed information if you want to plan a Big Trail adventure.

WHEN TO GO

Each route has a calendar indicating the best time to tackle the trail. Months (or half months) may be highlighted in the following colours.

Green – these are the best months to hit the trail. The entire route will be open; accommodation, food and public transport services will be operating at peak levels; normal weather conditions should not disrupt your trip.

Orange – it is generally possible to attempt the trail but it may require greater flexibility or better planning.

Some accommodation may be closed; other tourist services may also operate over reduced hours, if at all. Parts of the trail may be closed or diverted, and weather may mean that you are forced to abandon the trail.

Red – you should not tackle the trail unless you have significant skills and experience; you may have to be completely self-sufficient on the trail in challenging weather conditions; you may require winter mountain skills and all accommodation may be closed.

JAN	FEB	MAR	APR	MAY	JUN	JUL	AUG	SEP	OCT	NOV	DEC

THE DALES WAY FOLLOWS THE RIVER WHARFE AT BURNSALL. © STEPHEN ROSS

ICONS USED IN THIS BOOK

ACCOMMODATION

The accommodation icons highlight the different accommodation options available along the length of the trail. If there are a number of hostels along the trail, but you may have to spend one night in a bed and breakfast, the hostel icon will be shown. If there are hotels at the start of a trail, but none on, or close to, the rest of the route, the hotel icon will not be shown.

Camping – there are campsites on, or close to the route, or properties, such as hostels, that will permit camping nearby. This icon is generally not used to indicate wild camping, unless wild camping is legally permitted (or at least well-tolerated) and applicable to the route.

Bothies – these small, basic shelters are generally in mountainous or remote locations. Often they offer little more than a roof over your head – there may be no lights, toilet facilities or water, although some have a basic fireplace.

Hostels – budget accommodation is offered in shared dormitory rooms (and occasionally private rooms); often reduced rates are available to members of hostel associations. Although hostels vary greatly in the facilities they offer, the European hostelling movement grew out of walkers' and cyclists' need for affordable accommodation, so they are often located close to the trails and cater specifically for trail users.

Hotels – private rooms are offered, usually with en-suite facilities. In addition to breakfast, they will usually provide dining, and sometimes bar, facilities. They may offer additional services, such as laundry, a concierge and room service.

Bed and breakfasts or guest houses – s milar to hotels but may be smaller with more limited facilities. They will generally offer private rooms, which may be en-suite, and prices will include breakfast. Check-in times may be limited and if there is provision for evening meals, you may have to pre-order.

TRAIL CHARACTERISTICS

The trail characteristics icons provide information on the challenges that a trail presents.

Exposed – these trails offer little protection from the weather. You may be exposed to torrential rain, hot sunshine or dangerous thunderstorms. Exposed trails are often in mountains, and sometimes on ridges or mountain edges, so may also involve the risk of steep drops.

Remote – these trails are distant from towns, villages and roads. If you need to abandon the trail in an emergency, it may be challenging and take some time to reach help.

Steep – these trails have sections of sharp ascent or descent. Some ascents may be laddered, or may involve minimal scrambling. This icon is used to indicate where a trail has ascents or descents which may be technically challenging, rather than to identify trails with a lot of ups and downs.

Forest – these trails have sections through forests. Forest sections may be slippery, particularly during autumn leaf fall, and may present trip hazards. Navigation may be more challenging in forest sections as landmarks on the trail are obscured.

PATHS

The path icons indicate what type of tracks and paths you will generally encounter en route; for example, a trail may have a short road section but the road icon is only shown if roads make up a significant part of the route or if a long road section is encountered.

Roads – sections of the trail follow roads. There may be a pedestrian walkway, but you may also find yourself on the main carriageway next to traffic (although generally not on busy or main roads).

Open countryside – the trail crosses open countryside, with little or no indication of a path. You may need a map and compass to follow the trail, and the route may be boggy, bouldered or covered with vegetation.

Hard paths – the trail follows well-defined stone or tarmac paths; these trails are often on forestry tracks, or on trails shared with horse riders and cyclists. Stony or rocky paths may be slippery in wet weather, and if the surface is rocky or potholed may present a trip hazard.

Grassy paths – the trail follows well-defined grassy paths, often across pastures, but sometimes through woods or by rivers. The paths may be muddy, and sometimes narrow.

WAYMARKING

The waymarking icons indicate how easy or difficult the navigation is on the trail.

The trail is clearly waymarked along its entire length. You may need to pay careful attention to the waymarking where paths cross, or where there are trail variations. In good weather conditions, you should be able to follow the waymarked trail with minimal reliance on a map, guidebook or GPS route (although you should always have alternative means of navigation for emergencies).

The trail has some waymarking but you will probably need to navigate using a map, guidebook or GPS route on some or all of the trail. Some sections may be missing waymarks; waymarking may be out of date or poorly maintained; the route may only partially follow a waymarked trail.

There is no waymarking or very little waymarking on the trail. Some non-waymarked trails may also be remote and/or exposed, and you should be cautious about attempting these without significant trail experience. You will need to rely on good navigational skills to safely follow these trails, or you might consider hiring a guide or joining an organised holiday.

WALK, TREK, FASTPACK, RUN

Everyone tackles a Big Trail at their own pace, but in order to give you an indication of how long the trail may take, we have identified four user groups: *Walkers, Trekkers, Fastpackers* and *Trail runners*. The **Jones–Ross formula** has been developed that modernises and develops Naismith's rule to provide realistic timings for each user group.

All user groups move at different speeds and have a higher flat speed than ascent and descent speeds, but they also move at different rates in ascent and descent.

   Walkers move at a flat speed of around five kilometres per hour and move at very similar speeds while descending and ascending.

Trekkers move at a flat speed of around six kilometres per hour and move more quickly while descending than they do while ascending.

Fastpackers, who typically run on some sections of routes and walk on others, move at a flat speed of around eight kilometres per hour and move more quickly while descending than they do while ascending.

Trail runners move at a flat speed of around ten kilometres per hour and move far more quickly while descending than they do while ascending.

The trail timings (in days) are calculated assuming an average of around eight hours travelling on the trail per day.

CROSSING ONE MORE STILE ON THE PENNINE WAY. © SHUTTERSTOCK/DUNCAN ANDISON

A shorter day length of six hours is used to calculate the trail timings for Walkers for routes that may be tackled outside the summer months, when daylight hours are more limited. The Jones–Ross formula assumes average speeds – heavy kit, adverse weather conditions, your particular strengths in ascent or descent and tired legs may all impact on your actual pace.

The trail timings provided in this book are intended to provide an indication of time taken to complete the trail, assuming full days on the trail and no rest days. You might choose to tackle a Big Trail differently by, for example, running the trail in the morning and enjoying the local area in the afternoon or taking advantage of baggage services to let you walk longer and further each day. The accompanying guidebooks and guidemaps from Vertebrate Publishing, when available, provide all the information you need to tackle each Big Trail however you prefer. In a guidemap, the route is broken down into manageable sections, separated by timing points, allowing you to plan daily itineraries based on your user group, your own pace, and how long you want to spend on the trail each day. Each product provides information about food and accommodation at timing points, and suggested daily itineraries for each user group. As you follow the trail, you will quickly learn to adjust the timings provided by the Jones–Ross formula to fit your qualities of movement out on the trail.

The Jones–Ross formula in detail

Expressed in words, the Jones–Ross formula is:

$$\text{time} = \frac{\text{distance}}{\text{flat speed}} + \text{adjustment for ascent} + \text{adjustment for descent}$$

More precisely, it can be expressed as:

$$\text{time (minutes)} = \frac{\text{distance (km)}}{\text{flat speed (km per hour)}/60} + \frac{\text{vertical ascent (metres)}}{\text{vertical ascent speed (metres per hour)}/60} + \frac{\text{vertical descent (metres)}}{\text{vertical descent speed (metres per hour)}/60}$$

The flat speeds and vertical ascent and descent speeds for the four user groups are shown in Table 1.

	Flat speed (km per hour)	Vertical ascent speed (metres ascended per hour)	Vertical descent speed (metres descended per hour)
Walker	5	425	450
Trekker	6	450	750
Fastpacker	8	600	1000
Trail runner	10	1000	2000

TABLE **1**

PLANNING FOR A BIG TRAIL

PREPARATION

PICK YOUR TRAIL

Choose the trail that's right for you. Do you like mountains or coastal views, solitude or camaraderie? Do you want to run the trail, walk a fast trail or take time to enjoy the scenery? How many rest days do you want?

TAKE IT EASY

If this is your first Big Trail, don't make it any harder that it needs to be. Consider baggage transfer services to keep your day pack light. There's no better start to the day than a hearty breakfast, cooked by someone else, that will keep you satisfied all morning, so why not treat yourself to a bed and breakfast or hotel?

TEST YOUR KIT

Everyone, from your mum to the sales assistant to the grizzled thousand-kilometre hiker, will tell you the easiest way to complete the trail and the best way to avoid blisters. None of them are quite right. Find out what kit works for you – trail shoes or boots, flapjacks or protein bars, what socks, walking poles or not. Don't take kit that you haven't tested out on a long-distance trail – it's never great finding that your waterproofs aren't waterproof, or your tent is missing a pole, but it's easier if you can go home and come back another day! It's not just about boots, rucksacks and technical t-shirts – work out what you like to eat on the trail, and how much water you need to carry. Always wear your boots or shoes in well.

TRAIN

Get as many kilometres under your belt as possible. Carry the kit you plan to take with you. Hit the trail even when it's raining, or windy, or foggy and, if you can, try to get out on the trail two or more days in a row. Every hard-won kilometre of practice will make your time on the trail easier, but there are things that you can squeeze into a lunch hour that will also help. Sessions on an exercise bike can increase your cardiovascular fitness and improve aerobic performance; circuit training and high-intensity interval training can quickly develop core strength that will be invaluable when you're carrying a heavy day pack on a tricky path.

DEVELOP SKILLS

Hone your map reading and navigation skills. Practise route finding when there is no clear path. Learn how to pay attention to the developing weather, and the signs that will indicate the driest path through a bog.

PLAN

Any Big Trail is a challenge, but you can make it easier if all you have to concentrate on each day is following the trail. Book accommodation in advance; find out where you can get food and water on the trail; know your escape routes and know how to get help in an emergency. It's useful to know where you might buy replacement walking poles, new waterproofs or more blister plasters, and where there are cash machines. Rest days are not only a chance to recover; they're an excellent opportunity to restock, sort out kit and check out reports on the trail condition and weather forecast.

RECOMMENDED KIT LIST

Kit can be highly subjective and vary depending upon the person, the season and the level of experience or comfort. These recommended kit lists for walking or trekking can be adapted by fastpackers and trail runners, and are endorsed by our equipment partner **Alpkit** – the ideal resource for sourcing equipment for your adventure. ***www.alpkit.com***

KIT LIST FOR WALKING OR TREKKING
Safety
- Map and compass
- Whistle
- Mobile phone and charger (with plug adaptor, if required)
- Head torch (and spare batteries)
- Trekking poles
- First aid kit and blister kit

- Winter equipment (if required – crampons/micro-spikes, gaiters, ice axe)
- Tick removal kit

Essentials
- Toiletries and wet wipes
- Travel towel
- Travel wash
- Sleeping bag liner
- Sleeping mask
- Ear plugs
- Camera
- Sunscreen
- Insect repellent

Food and drink
- Water bottle
- Knife
- Snacks

Clothing
- Rucksack
- Waterproof rucksack liner
- Walking boots or trail shoes
- Waterproof jacket
- Waterproof trousers
- Walking trousers and shorts
- Wicking top x2
- Insulating layer
- Socks and underwear x2
- Gloves and warm hat
- Sunglasses
- Sunhat

Paperwork
- Passport and visas/Photographic ID
- Bank card
- Cash
- Proof of travel/activities insurance
- European Health Insurance Card, if applicable

Extra gear for camping or backpacking
- Tent/bivouac bag
- Sleeping mat
- Sleeping bag
- Stove
- Cooking gear and utensils
- Food
- Trowel

HIKING WITH CHILDREN

A Big Trail is the perfect way to begin a lifetime's love affair with outdoor adventure and can be the holiday that your children never forget. But a bad day on the trail with a disgruntled child may be the longest hours you'll ever experience. Plan, practise and don't forget you're supposed to be having fun.

Pick the right trail – look for child-friendly accommodation, plenty of places to eat en route and have shorter days without too much ascent. If your child is a baby or toddler, will you carry them or do you need a buggy-friendly path? Is the path safe for children? What else is there to do on the trail?

Take a break – plan plenty of refreshment stops and rest days.

Make it easy – investigate where you can take public transport to shorten days or skip boring road sections; consider baggage transfer; book catered accommodation.

Know your child – don't overestimate how far they can walk; understand what they find difficult or when they get tired; work out what cheers them up.

Look after yourself – don't forget that you'll have to carry at least some of your child's kit as well as your own. Plan for a heavy day pack with their spare layers, lunch and waterproofs. Don't overestimate your pace when you're hand-in-hand with a recalcitrant child.

SAFETY AND RESCUE

Always carry a **mobile phone** on the trail in order to alert emergency services in the event of an accident. Phone signal may be intermittent, particularly in remote or mountain areas. An SMS message may connect when voice calling is unavailable, and some local rescue services provide the option to contact them by text.

Do not rely on a single form of navigation. Mobile signals may be intermittent; electronic devices may be broken or lose charge; waymarking may be vandalised. It is advisable to always carry a map, and consider downloading GPX files to your navigation device.

Emergency services: 112 is the single EU emergency number and will connect you to emergency services in every European Union country, including Great Britain and Ireland. **999** is the British and Irish emergency number. Both 112 and 999 will also work on the Isle of Man.

In Great Britain, the emergency services can also be contacted by SMS text – useful if you have low battery or intermittent signal. Although primarily aimed at deaf and speech impaired people, EmergencySMS is available to anyone, if your service provider supports it, but it requires registration; you can register by sending an SMS message, 'register' to 999 (the UK) or 112 (Ireland). It is particularly useful in areas of the countryside where mobile signal is too weak to sustain phone contact but a text message might be sent. **EmergencySMS should only be used when voice call contact with emergency services is not possible.**

Mountain and other countryside rescue services in Great Britain and Ireland are provided as part of national emergency services and by voluntary organisations. Organisations such as Mountain Rescue are charitable organisations, financed by public donation and reliant entirely on volunteers.

In event of needing to call for rescue, prepare the following information.

Your name – normally you are asked your full name, and sometimes your address. Your mobile number will show on the emergency operator's screen, but you may be asked to confirm it.

Where you are – make sure you know how to locate your UTM coordinates using your mobile phone or smartwatch.

Phone number – if you are low on battery, tell the operator and provide an alternative phone number of another group member.

What occurred – detail the event that occurred in terms of numbers involved, their ages, and injuries and how they were sustained. Provide any detail you feel pertinent, such as fractures, medication, or the time elapsed since the accident.

Rescuer details – you may be asked various details that the rescue teams might require, such as local weather.

Try and remain calm when providing this information, as your clarity and quality of the information is of vital importance to the rescue team.

DISTRESS SIGNAL

The International (European) distress signal is **six blasts** of a **whistle** evenly spaced over **one minute**, followed by **a break of one minute**. Then **repeat**. The response that confirms that your signal has been received is three blasts of a whistle over one minute followed by a break of one minute. At night, flashes of a torch in the same sequence can be used instead. **Always carry a torch and a whistle.**

INSURANCE AND EMERGENCIES

It is essential that anyone planning a Big Trail obtains adequate insurance for their trip. Standard travel insurance policies often provide cover for low-level hiking routes, but you may be required to pay an extra premium for mountainous or remote trails.

LOOKING TOWARDS HOLYHEAD MOUNTAIN AND GOGARTH BAY FROM SOUTH STACK CLIFFS NATURE RESERVE ON THE ISLE OF ANGLESEY COASTAL PATH.
© JEN & SIM BENSON

THE
TRAILS

01 A DALES HIGH WAY – 143km

A Dales High Way, a new 143-kilometre route, traverses the stunning Yorkshire Dales from south to north, winding between market towns and villages and up over beautiful limestone hills. Unlike its better-known sibling, the Dales Way, it takes a high route across the countryside, tempting the walker to at least one peak on the fells on each day of walking. The trail, which was conceived by local walkers Tony and Chris Grogan in 2007, leads from Saltaire to Appleby-in-Westmorland and runs roughly parallel to the Settle–Carlisle Railway, enabling easy access to sections of the route from the railway.

Stepping off the train at Saltaire, you're immediately confronted with Salts Mill, Titus Salt's utopian mill, built with a vision of a better life for workers in Bradford's brutal textile industry. A working mill until 1986, it now houses many of local painter David Hockney's works, as well as shops and cafes. The route begins along the Leeds and Liverpool Canal but soon rises over the moors above Ilkley, passing the Twelve Apostles stone circle and the cup and ring Swastika Stone.

Skipton, the gateway to the Dales, is a charming market town with a twelfth-century castle. If you're lucky enough to pass through on market day, you can stock up for lunch with freshly baked bread and local cheeses. The route leaves Skipton with a stiff climb up the conical Sharp Haw. If you lift your eyes skyward, you may be fortunate enough to glimpse a red kite – these birds were successfully reintroduced to the area in the late 1990s.

You're never far on this route from the next tearoom where you can wash a slice of ginger parkin or curd tart down with a warm cup of strong Yorkshire tea. The area is also home to dozens of breweries – from the long-established Timothy Taylor to newer companies such as Saltaire Brewery. The Angel at Hetton, one of England's first gastropubs, won a Michelin star in the 2020 Michelin Guide, although you may need a brush and polish after a day's walking if you want to experience their award-winning food.

The Dales are walking country, and you'll find an abundance of bed and breakfasts, willing to dry your boots after a day in the hills. The hardiest of walkers will find plenty of camping spots on the route. At Malham, you might manage to squeeze into the always-popular Youth Hostel before your climb up Malham Cove. It is here that you will encounter the breathtaking cliffs, pavements and caverns of limestone country that so characterises the Dales.

At Settle, you might want to fortify yourself for the coming climb with a pitstop at Ye Olde Naked Man Cafe and Bakery. From Settle, A Dales High Way passes Stainforth (and the popular wild swimming spot of Stainforth Force) before entering Yorkshire Three Peaks country. The Yorkshire Three Peaks form a popular challenge route, that walkers aim to complete in under twelve hours, over Pen-y-Ghent, Whernside and Ingleborough – you can choose to take a variation to complete this challenge, although you might instead take the easier option and climb over Ingleborough and skirt the base of Whernside.

◀ LEAVING DENTDALE ON THE NORTHERN SLOPES OF WHERNSIDE.
© SKYWARE PRESS

Whichever way you decide to follow, the highlight of this section is the imposing Ribblehead Viaduct coming into view – you may even be fortunate enough to catch a glimpse of one of the steam trains that occasionally pass up and down the railway. In Chapel-le-Dale, you can see a memorial to more than 200 people who died during the construction of the railway from accidents or smallpox outbreaks – the churchyard here had to be extended to accommodate the unfortunate navvies, as well as their wives and children.

As you climb up over the Howgills, the landscape changes from limestone to slate and gritstone. The Howgill Fells are one of Britain's best kept secrets, beautiful wild hills so infrequently walked that, even on a bright summer's day, you might find yourself with only the hardy fell ponies for company. These are not the well-trodden paths and slabbed trails of the Lake District, but grassy trods across green giants. At the top of The Calf, the Howgills' highest point, on a clear day you can enjoy a panoramic view of the Lake District, and the Dales that you have just conquered.

Even as you near the finish, A Dales High Way still has surprises to delight you with – the bird-rich Sunbiggin Tarn, and then the expansive limestone pavement of Great Asby Scar. This area of Cumbria is one of the few remaining strongholds of the native red squirrel and, as you reach the Eden valley, you may glimpse them near the old mill at Rutter Force or in the grounds of Appleby Castle (now luxury accommodation and a popular wedding venue, although tours of the castle are available).

The route ends at the picturesque market town of Appleby, (in)famous for the Horse Fair, but at other times of year, an attractive Cumbrian agricultural town. You can claim a certificate of completion at Appleby's Tourist Information Centre. If you have time to spare at the end of your trip, you might want to climb nearby Cross Fell, one of England's highest peaks, and follow the Pennine Way along the ridge to the golf ball on Great Dun Fell.

ABOVE: HEADING FOR MALHAM COVE. © SKYWARE PRESS

BELOW: RIBBLEHEAD VIADUCT WITH INGLEBOROUGH BEHIND. © SKYWARE PRESS

INGLEBOROUGH VIEWED FROM RIBBLEHEAD VIADUCT. © JOHN COEFIELD

Appleby is a stop on the Settle–Carlisle Railway, and A Dales High Way is most easily started and finished by rail; the Settle–Carlisle Railway is one of the highest and most beautiful in the United Kingdom. Saltaire is on the Airedale line, well served by trains from Leeds and Bradford; Leeds Bradford Airport is the closest international airport, and Leeds is well connected by rail to other cities (London is approximately two hours and fifteen minutes away).

Yorkshire is God's own country, and the weather can feel apocalyptic. The walk may be attempted at any time of year, although winter conditions and short days present a challenge from October to April. Sunshine is never guaranteed and, as the route passes through high exposed moorland, be prepared for icy, freezing conditions in winter and rain and wind in summer. Even with a bright start, the peaks may still be obscured in mist. There is no surface more slippery than limestone pavement after a downpour, and it's worth remembering that a slathering of bog does wonders for the skin. But the verdant lushness of the Eden Valley, the timelessness of drystone walls lining high pastures, the sparkling waterfalls, and the wide blue bird-strewn skies will make you fall in love with this high route over the Dales. In spring you crush wild garlic in bluebell-rich woods, and in summer the moors glow purple with heather. On a fine day, this may be the brightest and most beautiful countryside you'll encounter in England.

01 A DALES HIGH WAY: ESSENTIAL INFORMATION

TRAIL ESSENTIALS

Start: **Saltaire, West Yorkshire, England**
End: **Appleby-in-Westmorland, Cumbria, England**
Distance: **143km**
Ascent/descent: **3,770m/3,690m**

HOW TO GET THERE

Saltaire is on the Airedale railway line, which connects to Leeds (where connections can be made to London, or coach connections to Leeds Bradford Airport).

Appleby is on the Settle–Carlisle Railway – there are direct rail connections from Settle to Leeds.

TIME TO COMPLETE

Walking: **8 days/46 hours**
Trekking: **5 days/37 hours**
Fastpacking: **4 days/28 hours**
Trail running: **3 days/20 hours**

PROS

• **The Howgills** – those that drive up the M6 to the Lake District may notice the Howgills on the other side of the motorway, but few stop to explore these green and golden fells. These tranquil hills, beloved by Alfred Wainwright, are Cumbria's best-kept secret.

• **Settle–Carlisle Railway** – this iconic railway, once puffed over by the Hogwarts Express, is known as one of Britain's highest and most spectacular routes. Many walkers choose to complete A Dales High Way and then enjoy a train ride back across the landscape they have just traversed.

• **Geology** – high on the moors, you'll pass the popular limestone pavement at Malham and a quieter twin near Great Asby. The Howgills have a distinctive Silurian sandstone that distinguishes their topography from the softer southern Dales and the jagged peaks of the Lake District.

CONS

• **Mist** – the Howgills may often offer beautiful views of the Lake District but, as often as not, you will find the summit views and grassy trods obscured by mist.

• **Tourist hotspots** – while much of A Dales High Way crosses quiet moorland, spots like Malham and Ribblesdale can attract thousands of daytrippers on sunny summer's days.

• **Appleby Horse Fair** – in early June, Appleby Horse Fair attracts approximately 10,000 members of the travelling community, and 30,000 other visitors to the small market town. Some local businesses close during the Fair. You are likely to experience difficulty finding accommodation and other services should your arrival in Appleby coincide with the Horse Fair.

GOOD TO KNOW

While the route only passes over Ingleborough, many walkers take a variation to complete all of the Yorkshire Three Peaks – Ingleborough, Whernside and Pen-y-Ghent. Every year, thousands attempt the Yorkshire Three Peaks route, including participants in one of England's oldest fell races, the Three Peaks Race – Andy Peace holds the men's record (two hours and forty-six minutes) and Victoria Wilkinson's the women's (three hours and nine minutes).

FURTHER INFORMATION

www.daleshighway.co.uk; the walk's creators, Tony and Chris Grogan, have written *A Dales High Way: Route Guide* (Skyware Press, 2020) and *A Dales High Way Companion* (Skyware Press, 2018).

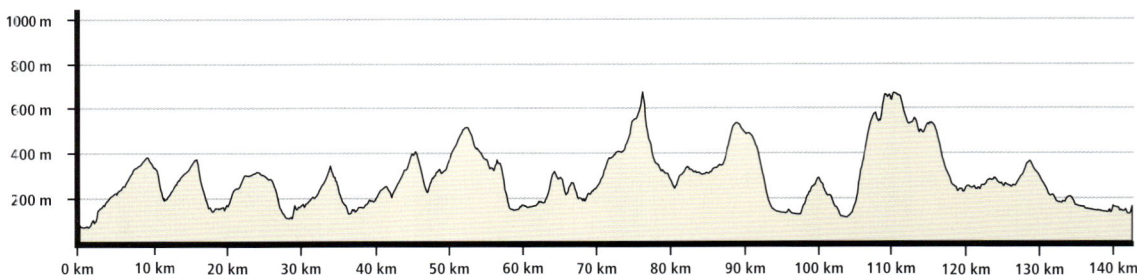

JAN	FEB	MAR	APR	MAY	JUN	JUL	AUG	SEP	OCT	NOV	DEC

CORK

02 BEARA WAY
– 211km

The Beara Peninsula is perhaps the remotest part of Ireland's wild Atlantic coast, a finger pointing into the ocean towards America. The sea here is sometimes so fierce that in 1881 it washed away the Calf Rock Lighthouse (six men were heroically rescued after being stranded on the rock for twelve days). Although not immune to the rain that makes Ireland so green, it is often unseasonably mild thanks to the Gulf Stream. Artists and poets have long been drawn to the isolated beauty of Beara, and Glengarriff, where the 211-kilometre Beara Way begins and ends, is renowned for traditional Irish music. *Ceol agus craic* in pubs aside, walkers may be tempted to linger for a few days in the village to enjoy the serene views of Bantry Bay, take a dip in the Blue Pool, and visit the Italian gardens on Garinish Island.

The Beara Way begins gently enough, with a stroll along the flower-lined Coomarkane River and on through ancient European oak woods. This is the Oakwood of the Blood that sheltered O'Sullivan, the last Irish prince of Beara, and his followers from the English in 1602. But the English captured his thousands of cows and sheep and, faced with starvation, a thousand men set off on a 500-kilometre march across Ireland – just thirty-five completed it.

Beara is a rugged peninsula and the route often climbs hills and over high, heathered, springy grassland. Ascents and descents are sometimes challenging, over slippery rocky trails, and sections may be boggy. After the woods, the route rises to a high pass beneath Sugarloaf Mountain, with fine views of hills, loughs and Bantry Bay. Descending, Toberavanaha Lough makes a fine lunch spot.

After a strenuous section, you'll be glad to reach Castletownbere. Once a treaty port, one of three that remained under British control after the founding of the Irish Free State, it's now Ireland's biggest fishing port. To truly complete the Beara Way, here you must take the ferry to walk a loop around Bere Island. Like the Beara Peninsula itself – which is home to more than 600 archaeological sites – the island is dotted with ancient standing stones and wedge tombs, alongside the newer Martello towers built to defend against Napoleon.

Back on the mainland, another rugged section brings you into (now defunct) mining country, with copper-green hued rocks and abandoned mine shafts. Once you conquer the steep and stony route, you'll reach the rainbow-painted houses of Ireland's remotest village, Allihies. Here there is another diversion from the mainland, and surely reason enough in itself to attempt this walk. From Dursey Sound, you must take Ireland's only cable car (and the only one in Europe to cross open seawater) to Dursey Island. They used to transport livestock across in the six-seater car but you no longer have to sway the 150 metres across with sheep at your knee or wait for a cow and calf to soar across.

From the island, you can view the remains of the Calf Rock Lighthouse and its replacement, Bull Rock Lighthouse, which was inhabited until it was automated in 1991. You may also be fortunate enough to see dolphins, whales or basking sharks. In 1602, the island was the site of the Dursey Massacre when 300 occupants of the O'Sullivan's

◀ ON THE FLANKS OF HUNGRY HILL.
© THOMAS BARTON

castle, mainly women and children, were shot with muskets or stabbed, and thrown from the cliffs.

From Dursey Head to Kenmare, the Beara Way is also the route of the European E8 trail, which you could follow for nearly 5,000 kilometres to Bulgaria (and eventually hopefully on to Turkey). It is a scenic start to the route with stunning cliff views, and then Eyeries, another multicoloured village awaits. The route stays low along stony beaches and dunes, passing from County Cork to County Kerry. At Ardgroom, you may diverge from the route to visit the Ardgroom Stone Circle but staying on the Way, soon enough, you'll climb along a medieval road to reach a pair of stone circles at Cashelkeelty.

From Lauragh, there's a short steep road section to Drombohilly. After Drombohilly, you pass Knockna-gorraveela, 'hill of the midges'. Unfortunately, the midges do not confine themselves to this hill – particularly in the summer months, you're likely to encounter them along the whole route. The route here may also be buzzing with tourists – the Uragh Stone Circle is one of the more popular sites on the peninsula.

The last town en route is Kenmare (although you may choose the more direct variation from Lauragh to Glen-garriff) – the Kerry Way also passes through here and bus services run from here to Killarney (and Cork, in the summer). Kenmare is famous for its restaurants, so you can try Bere Island mussels and scallops or Knockatee cheese. A quiet road climbs over the hills that bisect the peninsula, leading you back to the Glengarriff Woods.

Glengarriff is most easily reached by car, but daily bus services do run from Cork. In summer, buses run from Killarney (which can be reached by rail from Dublin)

DESCENDING INTO ADRIGOLE, ON BANTRY BAY. © THOMAS BARTON

to Kenmare, and from Kenmare to Glengarriff. International travellers arriving at Dublin can reach Cork by coach. There is little in the way of public transport on the peninsula itself, beyond the Bere Island ferry and Dursey Island cable car. Taxis and minibuses are available for hire and several companies offer baggage transfer; some walkers decide to hitchhike.

With the exception of Glengarriff and Kenmare, the route only passes through small villages with limited facilities. Though you may well find yourself the only person walking the Way, it is best to book accommodation in advance – your choices are moderately priced bed and breakfasts and small hotels. There are only a few campsites on the peninsula, but backpackers may find mountain spots or field corners (with the permission of landowners) to wild camp.

Glengarriff, a popular resort from Victorian times, claims to have the best climate in Ireland although this is perhaps a meagre claim. Even when it is not raining, a menace of damp tends to hang in the air. Standing stones more often than not will be wreathed in mist and you'll climb through clouds to reach the hill passes. But the fickle weather lends the sea a thousand different shades and, when the sun breaks through, the emerald moors glow.

Once upon a time, Beara was Ireland's wild west, popular with smugglers, outlaws and rebels. It is still a secret, untamed landscape with views to treasure. You'll walk in the shadow of mountains, through ash and birch and oak. In spring and summer, the hills drip with flowers, with fuchsia, hydrangeas, gorse and honeysuckle. This is Ireland as the locals know it, an Ireland few tourists are lucky enough to discover.

LOOKING BACK TOWARDS TRAIL START AT GLENGARRIFF. © JON BARTON

02 BEARA WAY: ESSENTIAL INFORMATION

TRAIL ESSENTIALS

Start:	**Glengarriff, County Cork, Ireland**
End:	**Glengarriff, County Cork, Ireland**
Distance:	**211km**
Ascent/descent:	**5,850m/5,740m**

HOW TO GET THERE

Glengarriff has daily bus connections to Cork, and in the summer to Killarney. Cork has an international airport, and weekly ferry services to France and Spain. Dublin and Belfast can be reached by rail from Cork or Killarney.

TIME TO COMPLETE

Walking:	**12 days/69 hours**
Trekking:	**7 days/56 hours**
Fastpacking:	**5 days/42 hours**
Trail running:	**4 days/30 hours**

PROS

- **Undiscovered** – while millions of tourists flock to Kerry to walk or drive the Kerry Way, its wilder neighbour, Beara, attracts only a handful of tourists, and few venture beyond Glengarriff.

- **Unusual transport** – the Beara Way is the only long-distance trail in the world that requires you to make a ferry journey and sway across the sea in a cable car in order to fully complete it.

- **Archaeology** – Beara is strewn with Bronze Age archaeology, and you will encounter wedge tombs, stone circles and standing stones en route, and more a short diversion away.

CONS

- **Midges** – there are at least twenty-nine species of tiny, blood-sucking midges in Ireland, and western Ireland has more than its fair share – you are most likely to encounter them in summer.

- **Public transport** – there are limited bus connections to Glengarriff in the summer, and very few in the winter. There is no public transport on the Beara Peninsula, other than the ferry and Dursey Island cable car.

- **No dogs** – the Beara Way traverses significant tracts of private land, and access has been agreed with landowners – one condition of that access is that dogs are not allowed on the Beara Way.

GOOD TO KNOW

Should you fancy an extra challenge, you might choose to detour from the Beara Way and climb into the remote Glenrastel valley. Hidden high in the hills is the cave of Pluais na Scriob – within the cave, a wall is etched with cuneiform, probably the oldest writing on stone in Ireland. No one knows exactly when it was carved, or what it means, and many of those who set out to find it fail in their search.

FURTHER INFORMATION

www.bearatourism.com/beara-way; Adrian's Hendroff's *The Beara and Sheep's Head Peninsulas* (Collins Press, 2015) provides useful information on the Beara Peninsula and describes several sections of the Way.

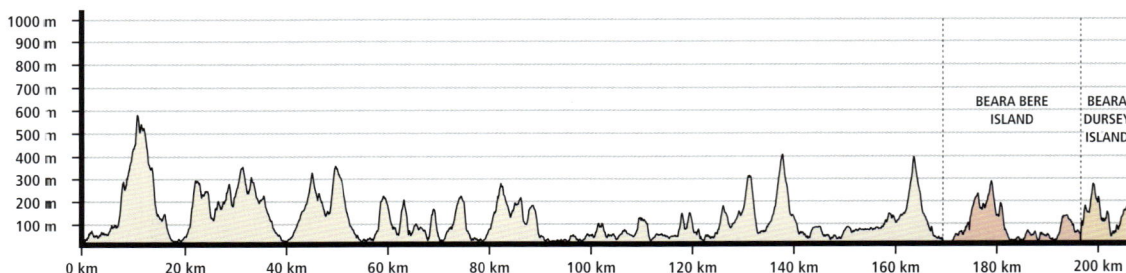

JAN	FEB	MAR	APR	MAY	JUN	JUL	AUG	SEP	OCT	NOV	DEC

IRELAND

Kilgarvan
Knockboy
Ballylickey
Bantry
Ballydehob

Knocknamanagh
R569
Kenmane
Killaha East
Gortlicka
Dawros
Templenoe

Glengarriff
N71
Sugarloaf Mountain
Barley Lake
Nareera

Durrus
Schull
Kilcrohane

Caha peninsula
Knocknagorraveela
Lough Inchiquin
Coomnadiha
Knockowen
Caha Mountains

R571
Clonee Lough Upper
Tuosist
Lauragh
R574

Aughgole
Derryclancy
Hungry Hill
Rerrin

Kenmare Bay
Castletcarty (stone circles)
Coomacloghane
Glenmore Lake
Lackabane
Eskataruff

Ballynakilla
Bere Island

Bantry Bay

An Carrán
Sneem
Coomcathoun
Knocknagantee

Ardgroom
Glenbeg Lough
Slieve Miskish Mountains
Maulin

Castletownbere

Eyeries
Kilcatherine

Derriana Lough
An Bheann Mhór
Coomcallee
Eagles Hill

Gullanore
Coulagh Bay
Knockoura
R572

Kealague
Killough

Caherdaniel
Ballaghaoherreen
Knocknagallaun
Allihies
Ballydonegan

Waterville
Lough Currane

Iveragh peninisula
Foilatough

Lackacroghan
Glanmore
Billeragh

Baile an Sceilg
Cabe Bar Link

Dursey Island

10 Kilometres

N

CARDIFF

03 CAMBRIAN WAY
— 462km

The 462-kilometre Cambrian Way traverses a whole country, from castle to castle, from capital city to the northern coast. You'll traverse some of Wales' wildest countryside, climb the highest mountain and walk from mountain to coast to mountain to coast. This route, the brainchild of Tony Drake, was fifty years in the making, and was once so controversial that the Brecon Beacons National Park banned the guidebook. Formally recognised in 2019, the Cambrian Way is not a well-paved, waymarked National Trail – it is an exposed, rugged adventure across the high lands of Wales, and a challenge even for the most experienced of walkers.

Beginning at the gates of eleventh-century Cardiff Castle, the Cambrian Way leaves the city by following the River Taff. At Whitchurch, you pass the Melingriffith Water Pump, all that remains of the tin works that were once the largest in the world. After the fairy-tale Gothic towers of the Victorian Castell Coch, you might be in for a big surprise as you venture into the woods because, just off the path, you'll find the honeycombed Three Bears Caves, the remnants of iron mining. The Way continues through dappled woods and along forestry tracks until you reach Pontypool.

On a clear day, seven counties are visible from the Folly Tower near Pontypool – this high tower was built in the 1760s, but demolished under the order of the Ministry of Defence in 1940, and reconstructed in the 1990s. As you leave Pontypool, you'll enter the Brecon Beacons. The flat topped, heather-swirled Blorenge, at 561 metres, is the first mountain you'll encounter en route before you descend in the pretty market town of Abergavenny.

After Abergavenny and the ascent up Sugar Loaf mountain, the route takes a dog-leg out to summit Lord Hereford's Knob, near the border with England, before traversing the high peaks of the Black Mountains on its return to Crickhowell. The traverse of the boggy, bracken-strewn uplands of the Brecon Beacons includes a climb up the 886-metre Pen y Fan, the highest point in South Wales. The stone-slabbed path up Pen y Fan is well travelled, but across the Beacons the path is often unmarked across grassy hilltops, and it is easy to become disorientated. You have a difficult choice between walking extra kilometres at the end of already long days to reach accommodation, or carrying all you need to camp high in the mountains.

The Cambrian Mountains are even wilder and more remote than the Brecon Beacons. The Ty'n Cornel Hostel, a nineteenth-century farmhouse, was one of a trio of remote, basic hostels sold by the YHA – the Elynydd Wilderness Hostels trust came to the rescue of two. Ty'n Cornel Hostel is the most remote hostel in Wales, eleven kilometres from the closest village, in the green Doethie Valley – Tony Drake, who pioneered the Cambrian Way in the 1960s, considered Doethie to be its most beautiful section.

The Doethie Valley's stream gives way to forest and then the route passes the twelfth-century Cistercian abbey, Strata Florida, before rising past the Teifi Pools, high in the Eleynydd, once described as the 'Green Desert of Wales'. This area of Elenydd sustained the last native population

◄ GLYDER FACH AND CASTELL Y GWYNT FROM GLYDER FAWR.
© THE CAMBRIAN WAY TRUST

of red kites in the United Kingdom; they have been flourishing in recent years.

At Devil's Bridge, the modern bridge built upon an eighteenth-century bridge built upon a medieval bridge, you can stop to admire the waterfalls. The Cambrian Way then climbs over the wild Plynlimon, the highest mountain in the Cambrian Mountains, on whose slopes the Wye and Severn both rise. You descend through bogs and abandoned mines to the welcome doors of the isolated Star Inn.

Near the grass-topped packhorse bridge of Pont Minllyn, you'll enter the route's final national park, Snowdonia. The highest challenge so far – 893-metre Cadair Idris, with its bottomless lakes, Snowdon's southern twin – faces you before you descend to the seaside town of Barmouth. The sandy beaches, in the shadow of Snowdonia's mountains, make Barmouth a popular resort for visitors from the West Midlands.

The scramble over the Rhinogydd mountains are the most challenging, although many would say the most spectacular, section of the route. The stone-slabbed Roman steps are not Roman, but rather a medieval packhorse route. A route over Wales' Matterhorn, Cnicht, takes you to Beddgelert, named for Prince Llewelyn's faithful dog.

Wales' highest mountain, the 1,085-metre-high Snowdon is your next challenge. Tackling Snowdon from the southern side, you turn from the Watkin Path to reach the Bwlch Main ridge, an exposed route up to Snowdon's summit. Most descend along the Pyg Track to Pen y Pass but some tackle the knife-edge arête of Crib Goch, a grade one scramble, as an alternative.

Though the highest summits are now behind you, even in its last day or two the Cambrian Way still has its views. The crossing of Glyderau offers the perfect photo opportunity, at the impossible rock platform of the Cantilever. One accommodation option here is YHA Idwal Cottage, a quarry manager's house near Llyn Ogwen that became one of the YHA's earliest youth hostels.

The rocky Carneddau Mountains must be crossed before the Cambrian Way descends to its finish in the walled town of Conwy. Home to one of Edward I's imposing castles, also offers the opportunity to view Thomas Telford's suspension bridge and Robert Stephenson's tubular railway bridge.

There are two ways to tackle the Cambrian Way: carry your tent and camp, sometimes wild camp along the route; or travel light and face blisteringly long distances as you detour off-route by up to ten kilometres to reach accommodation. While the route – which requires experience of mountain walking and navigation – may be attempted at any time of year, limited accommodation and the possibility of snow and ice on the higher sections make it more challenging between October and April. While many attempt the route in shorter segments – it is divided into southern, central and northern parts – it is not possible to access all sections of the route by public transport and strategic car-sharing may be your best option should you want to join or leave mid-route. Trains from Conwy travel to Holyhead, with its ferry port, or to Chester, where connections may be made to Manchester, Liverpool or Birmingham for international airports. Cardiff has an international airport, and good rail connections.

The Cambrian Way is not a waymarked route, not at least on the mountain heights. It is not a route at all, but rather forty-one checkpoints that must be reached in order to claim completion. The Cambrian Way is an opportunity for you not to follow in the footsteps of other walkers but to find your own way to cross a country, traversing its remotest mountains. You'll cross isolated high moors, and pass abandoned farms, chapels and mines. Like so many of Europe's best trails, the Cambrian Way arises out of walkers' passion for secret, wild places, known only to the explorers, and owes its existence to Tony Drake and the dedicated volunteers who followed him. The Cambrian Way is the route to attempt should you want to find Wales' wildest country, mountains wreathed in legend, and summits that, through the drizzle, open up wide, green vistas beneath your bog-stained, blistered feet.

TRAIL RUNNING IN THE BLACK MOUNTAINS. © JOHN COEFIELD

LOOKING ACROSS THE PYG TRACK TO SNOWDON SUMMIT AND GLASLYN. © JOHN COEFIELD

03 CAMBRIAN WAY: ESSENTIAL INFORMATION

TRAIL ESSENTIALS

Start:	**Cardiff, Wales**
End:	**Conwy, Wales**
Distance:	**462km**
Ascent/descent:	**17,540m/17,540m**

HOW TO GET THERE

Cardiff, Wales' capital city, has an international airport and good rail connections with Bristol and London.

Conwy is on the Holyhead–Crewe railway line. Connections to Cardiff may be made at Crewe, and Holyhead has a ferry port offering connections to Ireland.

TIME TO COMPLETE

Walking:	**29 days/173 hours**
Trekking:	**18 days/139 hours**
Fastpacking:	**13 days/105 hours**
Trail running:	**9 days/73 hours**

PROS

• **Mountains** – the Cambrian Way traverses all of Wales' mountain ranges: the Black Mountains, the Brecon Beacons, the Cambrian Mountains and the Rhinogydd. The route goes over Wales' highest peaks, climbing over Snowdon near journey's end.

• **Hostels** – the Cambrian Way passes two iconic hostels. Idwal Cottage, once a quarry manager's cottage, was the first property that the YHA acquired in Wales (in 1931) and is one of the YHA's oldest hostels. The wood-heated Elynydd Wilderness Ty'n y Cornel Hostel, once a farmhouse, is Wales' most remote hostel.

• **Dark skies** – the route passes through not one, but two, of the world's International Dark Sky Reserves (the Brecon Beacons and Snowdonia), making it the perfect route for ardent stargazers.

CONS

• **Accommodation** – when the route was devised, there were more hostels in the remote mountain areas. You may struggle to find accommodation in the remoter areas, particularly the Rhinogydd and Cambrian Mountains – and even campers may have to ask permission to camp in the corner of a farmer's field.

• **Meandering** – the route prefers the most challenging option to the most direct, and should you want to visit all the checkpoints, you may find yourself walking back on yourself. The land and access to it have changed since the route was conceived and some would argue that there are better alternatives for today's walkers.

GOOD TO KNOW

Another route that traverses Wales from north to south, crossing the same mountains as the Cambrian Way – climbing over Snowdon, and the Rhinogydd and Cambrian Mountains – is the Dragon's Back Race, possibly Britain's most brutal ultra. Run over five days, just like on the Cambrian Way, the runners have to find their own route over the mountains.

FURTHER INFORMATION

www.cambrianway.org.uk; *The Cambrian Way* (Cicerone, 2019).

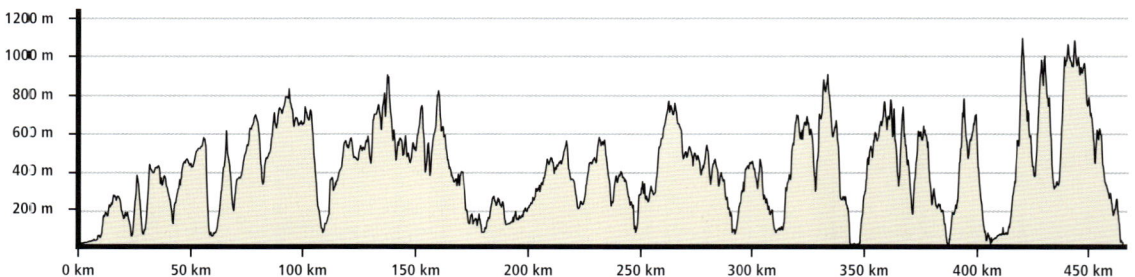

JAN	FEB	MAR	APR	MAY	JUN	JUL	AUG	SEP	OCT	NOV	DEC

Holyhead

Anglesey/
Ynys Môn

Warrington

Liverpool

Runcorn

Ellesmere Port

M56

M6

Rhyl

Colwyn Bay

Holywell

Saint Asaph

Bangor

Conwy

A55

A55

Chester

Caernarfon

Carnedd
Llewelyn

Snowdon/
Yr Wyddfa

Snowdonia
National Park

Betws-y-Coed

Ruthin

Clwydian Range and
Dee Valley AONB

Wrexham

Whitchurch

Beddgelert

Cnicht

Blaenau Ffestiniog

Maentwrog

Bala

A5

Llangollen

Chirk

Oswestry

Wem

Porthmadog

Abersoch

Harlech

Rhinogydd

Y Llethr

Dolgellau

A494

Cadair Berwyn

A529

A49

Barmouth

Cadair Idris

Mallwyd

A458

Welshpool

Shrewsbury

Telford

M54

Cardigan
Bay

Tywyn

Machynlleth

WALES

ENGLAND

A470

Borth

Plynlimon

Cambrian Mountains/
Elenydd

Newtown

Church Stretton

Bishop's Castle

Shropshire Hills
AONB

Craven Arms

Aberystwyth

Ponterwyd

Llanidloes

Clun

Ludlow

Kidderminster

Pontarfynach

Rhayader

Knighton

A456

Llan Ddu Fawr

Llandrindod

Aberaeron

Llanwrtyd
Wells

Builth Wells

Kington

Leominster

Cardigan

Lampeter

Rhandirmwyn

A483

Hay-on-Wye

A49

Hereford

Llandovery

A40

Talgarth

Lord Hereford's Knob /
Twmpa

Waun Fach

Carmarthen

Llandeilo

Black Mountain

Brecon

Pen y Fan

Black
Mountains

Abergavenny

M50

A40

Crickhowell

Brecon Beacons
National Park

Wye Valley
AONB

Monmouth

Pontardulais

Ebbw Vale

The Blorenge

Pontypool

Merthyr Tydfil

Cwmbran

Chepstow

River Severn

M48

M5

nby

Swansea

Pontypridd

Newport

M4

M4

Bristol

N

Cardiff

S

0   20 Kilometres

Barry

Bath

04 CAPE WRATH TRAIL – 378km

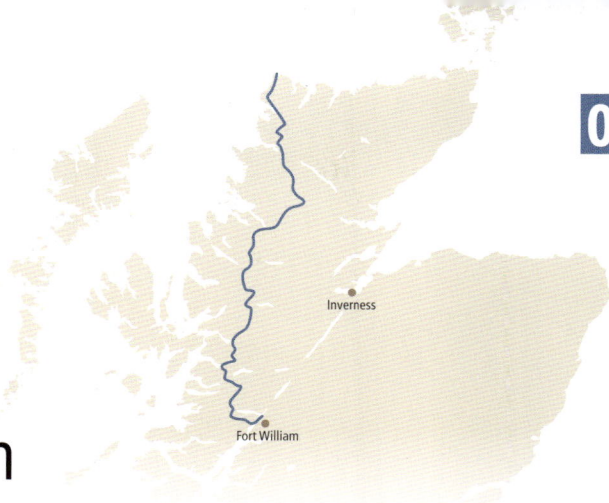

Inverness

Fort William

If you are in any doubt as to how challenging the 378-kilometre Cape Wrath Trail is, you just need to pause at the Commando Memorial at Spean Bridge – these remote Highlands are where the British Army still sends its soldiers to experience their toughest training. This trail – if you can call it a trail given that there is no single route, no waymarking and often no paths or track – is the toughest and remotest in the British Isles, and it is even a challenge for those who have built up years of experience. It is an adventure that will reward you with sandy beaches, the silhouette of a stag on heathered moorland, silent paths under snow-topped mountains. It is a trail where you will learn how little you will need and how much you can accomplish.

The trail begins at Fort William, Scotland's gateway to the Highlands. There are two different routes at the start. The Caledonian Canal variation follows the Great Glen Way along the Caledonian Canal, past Thomas Telford's Neptune's Staircase, a series of eight locks. Shortly after the Moy Swing Bridge, the only remaining example of Telford's cast iron bridges over the canal, you'll join a path that switches between the lochside and forest tracks at Loch Lochy and Loch Garry. As you cross into the glens above Loch Loyne and Loch Cluanie, you're inexorably heading towards the remote countryside. You'll get your feet wet both in the numerous bogs but also when crossing the River Loyne – you'll be glad of the hot food available at the isolated Cluanie Inn.

The Glenfinnan variation begins not on foot but with a short ferry ride over Loch Linnhe – you then immediately

head south, away from your final destination at Scotland's most north-westerly point. You follow the Cona River towards the Glenfinnan Monument to the 1745 Jacobite Rising, and then pass under the iconic Glenfinnan Viaduct. Built in 1897, it has featured on a Scottish banknote, and Harry Potter's Hogwarts Express steamed over it. After Glen Finnan, the route leaves stony trails behind and makes several grassy climbs over bealachs (low mountain passes). The Finiskaig River is the first of five rivers en route that must be forded. The Sourlies Bothy, perched on the shores of Loch Nevis, is one of Scotland's best-located bothies. Fortunately, you no longer have to ford the River Carnach as the disintegrating bridge was replaced in 2019.

The two variations converge at Morvich and immediately climb to the stunning Falls of Glomach, with their 113-metre drop – one of the highest in Britain. The stony path contouring around the gorge is treacherously slippery, particularly as it includes the fording of minor tributary waterfalls. After a tricky descent, a long hike through the green Glen Elchaig will lead you to what may be Scotland's remotest bothy, Maol-bhuidhe, which lies more than fifteen kilometres from any road.

You'll pass another (estate) bothy at Bendronaig and use the stalkers' path to climb Bealach Bhearnais – these mountain bothies, many maintained by the Mountain Bothies Association, are often on sporting estates, and access to them may be restricted during the stag stalking season from August to October.

◄ ONE OF THE BEST SECTIONS OF THE CAPE WRATH TRAIL, NEAR LOCHAN FADA ON THE APPROACH TO SHENAVALL BOTHY. © ALEX RODDIE

WILD CAMPING ON THE SHORE OF LOCHAN FADA — FIRE ON THE BEACH CLEARED AFTER USE. © WILL COPESTAKE

The trail continues through the Coulin Pass; the Old Pony Track, which leads to the pass, was an old drove track and was familiar to James Hogg, the Ettrick Shepherd, one of the first wilderness writers. After Kinlochewe, you will discover the Great Wilderness, the Fisherfields, a remote area far from human habitation. Shenavall Bothy is a popular base for exploring the Fisherfields. Although once a ferry crossed Loch Broom, now walkers have to hope to stop the bus near Inverlael, a village destroyed during the clearances, if they want to visit Ullapool.

Past the Knockdamph Bothy and the Duag Schoolhouse Bothy, in the shadows of the Beinn Dearg Munros, you'll reach the dappled salmon-fishing River Oykel. At Assynt, you might choose to detour to Scotland's largest cave system, the Traligill Caves. You'll pass the stunning Eas a Chual Aluinn, Britain's highest waterfall before you reach the Glencoul Bothy. Past the Glendhu Bothy, you'll encounter tracks for the forestry and hydroelectric projects (of Maldie Burn).

A grassy path leads up the Marilyn of Ben Dreavie – at 510 metres, this is the only summit crossed on the Cape Wrath Trail. This is a route that prefers the bealachs, or mountain passes, rather than the summits, but the trail still offers ascents and descents. The exposed, remote route is no less of a challenge for contouring the mountains that are the backdrop to the Cape Wrath Trail.

Through the peat moorland near Loch Aisir, owned by the John Muir Trust, the route reaches the freshwater Sandwood Loch. You arrive at the north-west coast at the golden sands, and dunes, of Sandwood Bay, a popular wild camping spot. This treacherous coast is home to mermaids, and it is said that the ghost of a shipwrecked mariner would knock on the window of the now ruined Sandwood Bay Cottage.

The final bothy en route is Strathchailleach Bothy, which was home to James 'Sandy' McRory-Smith for forty years – his illustrations still decorate the bothy walls. At the very end of the trail, at the end of Scotland itself, stands Cape Wrath Lighthouse, built in 1828 by Robert Stevenson (grandfather to the *Treasure Island* novelist, Robert Louis Stevenson). The nearby twenty-four hour Ozone Cafe is open every day.

KEARVAIG BOTHY ON THE NORTH COAST, JUST EAST OF CAPE WRATH. © WILL COPESTAKE

The trail is not waymarked, but you will often find yourself on stalkers' tracks, drovers' roads or even new tracks laid down for forestry or hydroelectric projects. However, the clearest trods can disappear into the bog and, while navigation may seem straightforward on sunny days with a clear view of the bealach that you're heading for, on a misty day you will be grateful for the occasional reassuring cairn. Though bridges now cross many of the burns, you may still struggle to ford rivers in spate.

Walkers on the Cape Wrath Trail must be prepared to camp. Although there are several bothies (and the occasional bunkhouse or hostel), these may be closed, particularly during lambing and the stalking season. They are now increasingly popular – where once you may have expected to share the fireplace with no one but a few mice, now, particularly in the summer months, you may find yourself in the company of other walkers and mountain bikers, and may be forced to camp outside the bothy (wild camping is permitted in Scotland). Those wishing to complete the trail should check that there is no firing on the army ranges at Cape Wrath. A (private) ferry and bus service runs, from May to September, to Durness – at other times, your only option may be to retrace your steps towards Kinlochbervie.

Cameron McNeish proposed a Scottish National Trail that traversed the length of Scotland from its border to its remotest coast, and now the Cape Wrath Trail is the end of that cross-country route. Through some of Scotland's most inhospitable terrain, you'll have to find your own way to reach the very edge of a country. From bothy to bothy, you will ford rivers, and bog-hop, searching for the right path over bealachs and by lochans, to reach a point that it is almost impossible to return from.

04 CAPE WRATH TRAIL: ESSENTIAL INFORMATION

TRAIL ESSENTIALS

Start:	**Fort William, Scotland**
End:	**Cape Wrath, Scotland**
Distance:	**378km**
Ascent/descent:	**11,010m/10,900m**

HOW TO GET THERE

Fort William is nearly four hours by train from Glasgow (the closest international airport). The Caledonian Sleeper offers an overnight, direct rail connection from Fort William to London (Euston).

For **Cape Wrath**, if you do not want to walk nearly twenty kilometres to Durness, you will have to take the private bus from the lighthouse to the Kyle of Durness, where there is a ferry to Keoldale Pier, near Durness. The bus and ferry connection only runs from Easter until October, and only when the weather permits. There is a bus service from Durness to Inverness, which has a train station and international airport.

TIME TO COMPLETE

Walking:	**21 days/126 hours**
Trekking:	**13 days/102 hours**
Fastpacking:	**10 days/77 hours**
Trail running:	**7 days/54 hours**

PROS

- **Bothies** – once a whispered secret, Scotland's bothies, most maintained by the Mountain Bothies Association, are in the wildest, remotest locations.

- **Remote** – this is perhaps Britain's most remote trail, even if it doesn't climb the mountains. Although increasingly popular, you will often find yourself alone on the trail, and far from human settlement.

- **Your challenge** – although most of the trail is on paths or tracks (some is not and requires navigation), you choose the paths you want to follow. There are several well-established variations, but you can choose an entirely different route. This is not a trail where you have to walk in anyone else's footsteps.

CONS

- **Transport** – connections to Cape Wrath are limited, and it is also difficult to reach other parts of the route by public transport.

- **Access** – you'll need to carefully time your travel. Rivers in spate may thwart your journey, and paths may be blocked at high tide. Bothies may be unavailable during stalking season, or when needed by farmers. Cape Wrath may be closed at twenty-four hours' notice for military exercises.

- **Heavy packs** – the trail is remote, and you'll need to carry plenty of food and, even if you plan to trek from bothy to bothy, you will need cooking equipment and would be well-advised to carry camping kit in case of bad weather or full bothies.

GOOD TO KNOW

In 2018, Damian Hall and Beth Pascall set a new fastest known time for completing the Cape Wrath Trail in four days, nine hours and forty-three minutes, knocking three days off the previous record. Not satisfied with just tackling Britain's toughest trail, they decided to make their attempt on the record in December, when there are only six hours of daylight per day.

FURTHER INFORMATION

The Cape Wrath Trail (Cicerone, 2015).

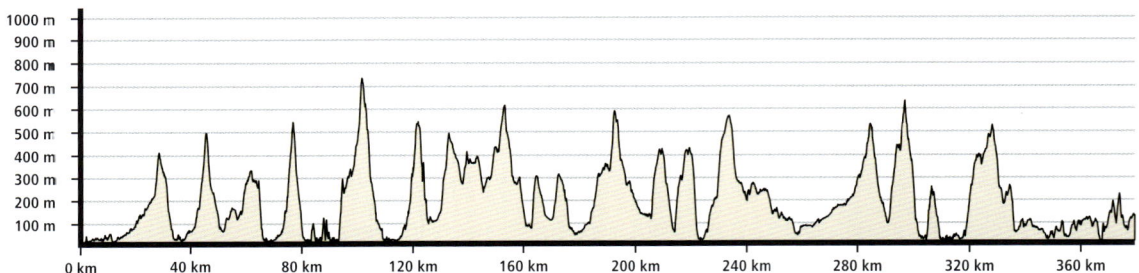

JAN	FEB	MAR	APR	MAY	JUN	JUL	AUG	SEP	OCT	NOV	DEC

Cape Wrath F

Bay of Keisgaig

Durness

Bettyhill

Melvich

Blairmore

Kinlochbervie

Achriesgill

Scourie

▲ Arkle

Ben Dreavie

Kylestrome

▲ Beinn a Bhùtha

Stoer

Lewis

Stornoway

Inchnadamph

▲ Conival

Assynt-Coigach

Lairg

Rosehall

Gob na Foide

The Minch

Ullapool

Cnoc Damh

Ardgay

Dornoch

Tain

Laide

Dundonnell

Meall Dubh

An Teallach

Inverlael

▲ Beinn Dearg

Gairloch

Wester Ross

▲ Sgùrr Mòr

Tom a'Choinnich

Alness

Invergordon

Sidhean Biorach

Kinlochewe

Achnasheen

Dingwall

Fortrose

Beinn Eighe

Nairn

Craig

▲ Càrn nan Gobhar

Muir of Ord

Strathcarron

Bidean an Eoin Deirg

Inverness

Portree

Skye

Inner Sound

An Riabhachan

Cannich

Kyle of Lochalsh

Càrn Eige ▲

Inverinate

Broadford

Morvich

▲ Beinn Fhada

SCOTLAND

The Cuillin

Invershiel

▲ A'Chràileag

Glenelg

Caolasmór

Kinlochhourn

Fort Augustus

Aviemore

Barrisdale

Loch Garry

Invergarry

Kingussie

▲ Sgùrr na Cìche

Garrygualach

Glendessary

South Laggan

Mallaig

Loch Nevis

Bunarkaig

Creag Meagaidh ▲

Gairlochy

Glenfinnan

S Fort William

Salen

Strontian

Loch Linnhe

Ben Alder ▲

Pitlochry

N

0   20 Kilometres

05 CAUSEWAY COAST WAY — 53km

Londonderry/
Derry

BELFAST

Not every big trail has to be a big ordeal, or an epic thirty-day slog through the mountains. If you want a short trail that packs scenery in around every corner and that will let you discover the soul of a country in a long weekend, then the fifty-three-kilometre Causeway Coast Way along the northern shores of Northern Ireland is the route for you. Starting in the charming coastal town of Port-stewart, where you can enjoy the *craic* and the local seafood, you'll pass through scenery so dramatic that it steals the limelight in films and television shows. You can enjoy a dram at Bushmills and step out on to the legendary Giant's Causeway before finishing at the white-washed cottages of seaside Ballycastle. Escape to the seaside, the very best of it, just as you remember from childhood.

The Causeway Coast Way starts at Portstewart, by the entrance to the beautiful Portstewart Strand. The three-kilometre beach, with its fragile dunes, is owned by the National Trust and was voted the UK's best Blue Flag Beach in 2016. If you want to ensure good luck for your walk, you should take a short detour from the start, behind the clifftop bungalows, to St Patrick's Well. The Way follows the cliff path around the edge of the championship-hosting Portstewart Golf Club — this club actually has three courses, making it one of a handful of fifty-four-hole clubs in Europe.

Portrush, home to the Royal Portrush Golf Club, which last hosted The Open in 2019, is one of Northern Ireland's most popular seaside towns. With its award-winning beaches and Barry's Amusements, the largest amusement park in Northern Ireland, this is a great place for an ice cream

pitstop. If you arrive in Portrush on a Saturday you could join in the five-kilometre Parkrun along East Strand Beach — it was the first Parkrun in the world to be run entirely on sand.

Leaving the twin resorts of Portrush and Portstewart behind you, the Causeway Coast Way opens into sandy beaches beneath limestone cliffs. You can choose to walk along the beach, pausing for an invigorating swim, or enjoy the views from the flower-lined clifftop path. Just before you reach Portballintrae you can make a short detour to visit the clifftop ruins of the sixteenth-century Dunluce Castle — local legend claims that the castle kitchens tumbled into the sea during a storm, with the only survivor being a kitchen boy who had been resting by the fire. You can climb the steps down the precipitous cliffs to peer into the gaping Mermaid Cave.

After the beauty of the cliffs, the route into pretty Portballintrae is an unfortunate roadside slog. From Portballintrae, you can continue along the coast or turn slightly inland towards Bushmills, home to the Old Bushmills Distillery. The distillery site has been licensed since 1608, giving it some claim to being the oldest licensed whiskey distillery in the world. From Bushmills, you follow the route of the Giant's Causeway Tramway — tourist trains still run on this line between Bushmills and the Giant's Causeway, although the route once extended much further to Portrush.

◀ WHITEROCKS BEACH, LOOKING BACK TOWARDS PORTRUSH.
© HENDRIK MORKEL/WWW.HIKINGINFINLAND.COM

DUNLUCE CASTLE. © HENDRIK MORKEL/WWW.HIKINGINFINLAND.COM

One of the natural wonders of the world, the hexagonal basalt columns of the Giant's Causeway stretch out into the Irish Sea; according to legend, they are the remains of the bridge to Scotland built by the giant Finn MacCool. Although the Way remains on the clifftops, bypassing the Causeway, few do not take the short diversion down to the shore to see the stone road disappearing into the waves. A steep climb up the Shepherd's Steps will take you back to the clifftop path.

At Port na Spaniagh, the wreck of the gold-laden *Girona*, one of the ships of the 1588 Spanish Armada, still lies beneath the sea – divers found it in 1967, and you can see the coins and jewellery recovered from it in the Ulster Museum. Walkers pass, but cannot stay at, the Port Moon Bothy – this basic hut, maintained by the Causeway Coast Kayak Association, can only be reached by sea. On a clear day from these clifftops, you can see Scotland's coastline. The Way meanders along the clifftops, past the remains of Dunseverick Castle, once a place of pilgrimage for St Patrick, towards White Park Bay. The church in a converted cow byre, St Gobban's, was once the Ireland's smallest church but was demolished in 2017.

The trail makes a steepy, stony scramble to the beach at White Park Bay, passing through an arch in the cliffs themselves, although if the tides are high you may have to detour along the A2 road past the White Park Bay Hostel. The path leads, past sea stacks and arches, to the pretty harbour of Ballintoy – this once quiet village doubled as the Isle of Pyke in *Game of Thrones*.

You may wish to leave the Causeway Coast Way again to totter across the Carrick-a-Rede rope bridge. Once little more than rickety planks with a single guide rope, the first bridge was erected here by fishermen in the 1750s – you can still see the fisherman's cottage. The current, sturdier rope bridge was installed in 2008, but it may still be closed in high winds. Carrickarede Island offers fine views across to the lighthouse on Rathlin Island.

Back en route, the rocky sides of Larrybane Quarry served as Renly Baratheon's camp in *Game of Thrones*. The route into Ballycastle, where the Causeway Coast Way ends, has been diverted along the quieter Glenstaughey Road rather than the busy B15, but it is an inauspicious end to a beautiful route – negotiations are under way to secure a pleasanter coastal alternative to this short road section.

CLIFFTOP MARKER NEAR THE GIANT'S CAUSEWAY. © HENDRIK MORKEL/WWW.HIKINGINFINLAND.COM

The Causeway Coast Way is a short, and arguably the best, section of the 1,000-kilometre Ulster Way. Encircling the counties of Ulster, the Ulster Way is one of the lengthiest long-distance trails in the British Isles, and offers stunning sections through Northern Ireland's verdant mountains and shining coast, but the link sections are often along busy roads. If you want to 'complete' the trail, the Ulster Way may not be the most satisfying of challenges, but if you want to find day or weekend walks, the quality sections of the Ulster Way are ideal, and are well waymarked.

The route may be walked at any time of year, although bus services will be more limited and attractions may close or offer shorter opening hours in the winter months. Belfast's airports offer flights to the UK mainland, as well as international flights, and ferries operate between Northern Ireland and England (Liverpool) and Scotland (Cairnryan). You'll find welcoming bed and breakfast accommodation on the route, as well as some hostels and campsites.

Too few tourists visit the friendly, energetic city of Belfast, and fewer still discover Northern Ireland's beautiful coast. The Causeway Coast Way will reveal stunning cliff views, crumbling castles and one of the world's natural wonders, the Giant's Causeway. This walk is perfect for you if you want a long weekend of easy walks, spectacular views and picturesque villages. You can start each day with a hearty Ulster fry, enjoy lunch by the harbour, feast on fresh seafood and finish each day with a Bushmills nightcap.

05 CAUSEWAY COAST WAY: ESSENTIAL INFORMATION

TRAIL ESSENTIALS

Start:	**Portstewart, County Londonderry, Northern Ireland**
End:	**Ballycastle, County Antrim, Northern Ireland**
Distance:	**53km**
Ascent/descent:	**740m/760m**

HOW TO GET THERE

Portstewart offers bus services to Coleraine, where bus or rail connections can be made to Belfast. Belfast has two international airports, and also ferry services to England and Scotland. The smaller City of Derry Airport is also close to Portstewart.

Ballycastle has bus services to Ballymena, where rail and bus connections can be made to Belfast. You may find public transport services to the Causeway Coast run infrequently, particularly outside the summer season, and travel by taxi or private car may be the most practical option.

TIME TO COMPLETE

Walking:	**3 days/14 hours**
Trekking:	**2 days/12 hours**
Fastpacking:	**2 days/9 hours**
Trail running:	**1 day/7 hours**

PROS

• **Giant's Causeway** – the Causeway, considered by many to be one of the natural wonders of the world, is approximately 40,000 interlocking basalt columns, the result of an ancient volcanic eruption. Although some may tell you that it is the remains of the bridge that the giant Finn MacCool built, to fight the Scottish giant Benandonner.

• **Ulster Fry** – there is no finer breakfast to start a walker's day than the Ulster fry – the traditional fried breakfast of bacon, sausage and egg, accompanied by soda farl and potato bread.

• *Game of Thrones* **views** – the twisted forests, dramatic coasts and cliffs, and green mountains of Northern Ireland were the perfect scenic backdrop for the television epic *Game of Thrones*. On the trail, ardent fans may recognise Lordsport Harbour, the coast of Dorne and Renly Baratheon's camp. After your walk, you may want to take a trip to the beech-arched roads of Dark Hedges, also known as Kingsroad.

CONS

• **Busy roads** – although there is now a quieter, still on-road, route into Ballycastle, there is also a tedious road section into Portballintrae.

• **Quality not quantity** – at only ten kilometres longer than a marathon, the Causeway Coast Way is not the trail to walk if you want to walk further, faster or harder than your friends. It is not a trail of fierce challenges, long distances or early starts. It is the ideal first trail, great for morning walking and afternoon sightseeing, and the perfect relaxed trail for a long weekend.

GOOD TO KNOW

The Causeway Coast Way is a section of the 1,000-kilometre Ulster Way which passes through the six counties of Northern Ireland, encircling the country. First conceived of in the 1940s, it was launched in the 1970s and relaunched in the 2009, after it had fallen somewhat into neglect and disuse. The reimagined Ulster Way is not a true loop – it is quality sections, like the Causeway Coast Way, connected by link sections, often on busy roads. This makes the Ulster Way a perfect route to dip in to.

FURTHER INFORMATION

www.walkni.com/walks/causeway-coast-way

JAN	FEB	MAR	APR	MAY	JUN	JUL	AUG	SEP	OCT	NOV	DEC

Church Bay

Rathlin Island

Rathlin Sound

Atlantic Ocean

NORTHERN IRELAND

Ballyvoy

Antrim Coast & Glens
AONB

Ballycastle Bay

Ballycastle

Kinbane Head

Carrick-a-Rede rope bridge

Ballintoy

Ballintoy Harbour
Boheeshane Bay

White Park Bay

Portbradden

Dunseverick Castle
Dunseverick

Causeway Coast
AONB

Giant's Causeway

Portnaboe

Runkerry Strand

Portballintrae

Dunluce Castle

The Skerries

Portrush

Portstewart

Portstewart Strand

Binevenagh AONB

Cape Castle

Armoy

Knocklayd

Greaghan

Loughguile

B15

A44

B67

B147

Moss-Side

Stranocum

Dervock

B17

B66

Bushmills

A2

Ballybogey

Ballymoney

Balnamore

A26

Coleraine

Lower Bann

A29

A2

Macosquin

B17

B201

Articlave

Berock

A44

N

5 Kilometres

0

06 CLEVELAND WAY – 174km

The 174-kilometre Cleveland Way is a unique Yorkshire trail, from Helmsley to Filey, that first traverses the moors of North Yorkshire before tracing the beautiful coastal clifftops. The first half of the trail crosses the high, wild North York moors, once busy with industry, now eerily quiet except for a few pretty villages. The second half explores the sandy beaches, hamlets nestled under the cliffs, and Victorian seaside resorts of the Yorkshire coast. This is a dramatic coastal landscape, of soaring cliffs, that inspired painters and writers. Steep climbs and wooded descents to the beach will merit an ice cream on the Staithes or Whitby's pretty seafront.

The Rye Valley gives its name to the ruined Rievaulx Abbey, which you pass on the route – this Cistercian abbey was founded in 1132, and reduced to ruins by Henry VIII's Dissolution of the Monasteries. Edward II was having dinner here when he heard news that the Scots had defeated the English army at the Battle of Scawton Moor in 1322 – he had to flee, forgetting the royal treasure (and the Great Seal of England). The Scots subsequently sacked the abbey, but thoughtfully returned his seal.

The panoramic views of Yorkshire from Sutton Bank are among the best on the walk. The tall cliff provided the ideal location for one of Britain's earliest gliding clubs, and it was here that Amy Johnson honed her flying skills. The gliding club acquired a horse, Major, in 1938 to retrieve the gliders, but after a close miss during a landing, the horse refused to go anywhere near them.

◄ LOOKING BACK ALONG THE CLIFFS TOWARDS ROBIN HOOD'S BAY.
© SHUTTERSTOCK/PETE STUART

Horses have always been important on these hills – Hambleton Racecourse was once only second to Newmarket. In 1857, a schoolmaster carved England's most northern white horse into the Kilburn hillside – the Cleveland Way takes a short detour to visit it. Some say that it is the white horse from the legend of Gormire Lake (which you can see from Sutton Bank). An abbot and a squire were racing on horseback, but the abbot suddenly changed into the devil, and in astonishment the squire plunged into the lake. The devil followed him, turning the lake waters inky black. Gormire Lake is now a popular wild swimming spot, although also renowned for the leeches lurking in its shallow waters.

The Way follows a grassy drovers' track over the limestone Hambleton Hills – used from prehistoric times, it became a popular route with eighteenth and nineteenth-century Scotsmen driving their cattle to English market towns. After the pretty village of Osmotherley – with its own religious ruin, Mount Grace Priory, the best-preserved Carthusian monastery in England – the Cleveland Way and Coast to Coast routes coincide, and the Cleveland Way reaches its wildest, most challenging, moorland section.

On heather moorland, you'll climb to the jagged outcrop of the Wainstones. Although the landscape laid out before you appears wild, it is one that has been sculpted by the extensive ironstone and alum mining that that has occurred over centuries. The highest point on the Way is at Urra Moor, where a trig point on top of an Iron Age barrow, marks the 454-metre summit. At Bloworth

THE RUINS OF WHITBY ABBEY. © CONTOURS HOLIDAYS

Crossing, you'll pass the remains of an old mining railway. Stone markers – some boundary markers, some waymarkers, some so old that no-one know their purpose – dot the moors here; the face marker is Celtic and the hand marker an old guide marker pointing the way to Ingleby and Guisborough.

A taller waymarker, Captain Cook's Monument, a massive obelisk erected in 1827 atop Easby Moor, also guides you. From the summit of the nearby Roseberry Topping, Yorkshire's Matterhorn (although only 320 metres high), you might catch your first glimpse of the sea.

The dappled Guisborough Woods lead you to the coast at Saltburn-by-the-Sea, a Victorian holiday resort. Saltburn is still a pleasant seaside town, with plenty of beachside cafes to lunch in, a funicular trundling up and down the cliff, and the only surviving Victorian pier on the north-east coast.

The remainder of the Cleveland Way follows the clifftops and beaches of Yorkshire's coast. Just before Staithes, Boulby Cliff is the highest point, at 203 metres, on the east coast; nearby Boulby Mine, a potash mine and the second deepest mine in Europe, hosts a laboratory 1,100 metres underground. Staithes is a pretty fishing village, tucked into the gorge carved out by Roxby Beck – once home to a colony of artists, it's now where *Old Jack's Boat* is filmed. You have to time your departure from Staithes to ensure that you can cross Runswick Bay before high tide.

If you wish to avoid the tourists thronging Whitby's narrow streets, you can pause at Sandsend for a cream tea – it's a pleasant five-kilometre walk along golden sands into Whitby, the harbour town famous for *Dracula* and black jet. The path crosses the busy River Esk and climbs 199 steps, past St Mary's Church and the ruins of Whitby Abbey (now adjacent to a youth hostel) to regain the cliff path towards Robin Hood's Bay.

Just outside the smuggler's haunt of Robin Hood's Bay, a wooden post stands on the clifftop, a replica of the rocket post that once stood here. From here, ropes were fired to stranded ships so that the crews could be hauled ashore – in 1936, the crew of the steamship *Heatherfield*, and the captain's canary, were rescued.

THE PATH TO THE SUMMIT OF ROSEBERRY TOPPING. © CONTOURS HOLIDAYS

Coast-to-coasters finish their journey at Robin Hood's Bay, but the Cleveland Way climbs up the cliffs before dropping to the beach at Boggle Hole, where a youth hostel nestles at the back of the beach. Past the town that never was, Ravenscar, the waterfall at Hayburn Wyke is a hidden beauty – here the path drops to the beach briefly, before climbing through bluebell woods.

Although Scarborough is a town whose seaside charms have faded somewhat, you can still admire the ruins of the castle and the grand Victorian Spa at South Bay. The Cleveland Way climbs to the cliffs and follows grassy high paths, past the golden sands of Cayton Bay and through a caravanned holiday park, to reach journey's end at Filey Brigg.

The Cleveland Way can be walked at any time of year, although in winter the moors may be covered in snow, drenched in rain or wreathed in mist, and you will feel the exposure of the high cliff paths. Helmsley may be reached by bus from York, and Filey is on the Hull–Scarborough rail route. There are plenty of bed and breakfasts en route, as well as youth hostels, and campsites (in summer).

The coastline is highly susceptible to landslides so the path may be diverted, and you should be wary of straying too close to the cliff edge.

The Cleveland Way offers a unique combination of Yorkshire moorland, and beautiful coast paths. After a hard day's walk, you can reward yourself with a seafood supper sitting on the cobbled harbour of a fishing village. These are also the paths where the Hardmoors ultra races are run, and although the drops down to (and up from!) the beach may leave you gasping for breath, the cool sea breezes will make the run over grassy, undulating clifftop trails heavenly. You're never too far from an ice cream stop in a bustling resort, and closer still to the next deserted beauty spot.

TRAIL ESSENTIALS

Start: **Helmsley, North Yorkshire, England**
End: **Filey, North Yorkshire, England**
Distance: **174km**
Ascent/descent: **3,600m/3,630m**

HOW TO GET THERE

Helmsley has frequent bus services to York. York offers mainline rail services to other English and Scottish cities. The closest international airport is Leeds Bradford Airport.

Filey is on the regional Scarborough–Hull railway line – connections may be made to mainline railway services via York. Hull also offers ferry connections to continental Europe (Belgium and the Netherlands).

TIME TO COMPLETE

Walking: **9 days/51 hours**
Trekking: **6 days/42 hours**
Fastpacking: **4 days/32 hours**
Trail running: **3 days/23 hours**

PROS

• **Seaside towns** – Saltburn-by-the-Sea retains its Victorian charms, but also offers great modern dining. Staithes is a picture-perfect fishing village. Visit Whitby for its seafood, particularly lobsters, and Scarborough for the guilty seaside pleasures of penny arcades, and fish and chips on the promenade.

• **Birds** – the most avid ornithologists might wish to carry on past Filey to Flamborough's famous cliffs, but the Yorkshire cliffs will still offer you the opportunity to view great cormorants, shags, guillemots and puffins. Over the moors, you might see grouse, curlews, and perhaps even the golden plover.

• **Moors and cliffs** – some routes cross moors, some trace coastlines. Some journey from coast to coast. The Cleveland Way is one of the few that offers days across countryside, followed by days on the coast.

CONS

• **Mist** – Dracula's arrival in Whitby is heralded by a sudden, violent storm, accompanied by 'a mass of dank mist ... like a grey pall'. Author Bram Stoker, who visited in 1890, obviously encountered the dense mists that can envelop Yorkshire's coasts and moors with little warning.

• **Diversions** – the clifftop paths are susceptible to landslips and are often diverted. Moorland fires and occasional flooding have also caused disruption to the route. You will have to take a lengthy roadside diversion if you arrive at Runswick Bay at high tide.

• **Ups and downs** – These are the highest cliffs on the north-east coast, and cliffs that have been divided by river gorges. You'll face plenty of steep stony paths and steps up and down from beach to cliff to beach again.

GOOD TO KNOW

The Hardmoors ultra races follow the Cleveland Way over moors and coast paths. A half marathon, marathon and five ultra races are run. Hardmoors 110 covers the whole of the Cleveland Way and offers six UTMB qualification points.

FURTHER INFORMATION

www.nationaltrail.co.uk/en_GB/trails/cleveland-way

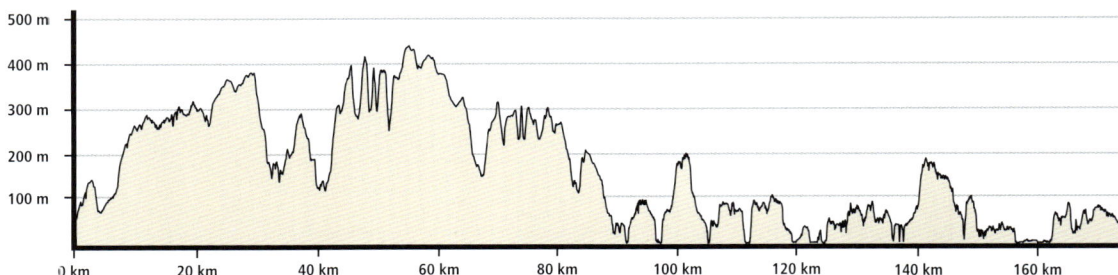

JAN	FEB	MAR	APR	MAY	JUN	JUL	AUG	SEP	OCT	NOV	DEC

North Sea

ENGLAND

North York Moors National Park

Bridlington

Filey
Filey Bay
Hunmanby

Cayton Bay
South Bay
North Bay
Eastfield

Scarborough

Burniston
East Ayton

Robin Hood's Bay
Ravenscar

Whitby
Sandsend
Sleights

Kettleness
Runswick Bay
Staithes
Boulby

Skinningrove
Loftus

Saltburn-by-the-Sea
Brotton
Skelton Green
Skelton-in-Cleveland
Slapewath

Redcar

Guisborough

Kildale

River Esk

Seavey Hill
Ledging Hill
Stony Ridge
Bloworth Crossing

Roseberry Topping
The Wainstones
Round Hill

Kirkbymoorside

Pickering

Malton

Helmsley
Rievaulx Abbey

Cold Kirby
WhiteHorse
Sutton Bank

Chop Gate

Black Hamleton

Osmotherley
Swainby

Stokesley
Hutton Rudby

Middlesbrough
Stockton-on-Tees
Ingleby Barwick
Yarm
Billingham

Thirsk

River Tees

A19 A66 A174 A172 A171 A169 A170 A64 A19

10 Kilometres

N

Cheltenham
Gloucester •

BRISTOL
BATH

07 COTSWOLD
WAY – 168km

**Rolling hills, gentle farmland, honeyed-stone
cottages; the Cotswolds are classic chocolate-box
country, almost unchanged in character since Laurie
Lee wrote his bucolic memoir, *Cider with Rosie*.
The 168-kilometre Cotswold Way stretches from
Chipping Campden in the north to the elegant city
of Bath and, while you'll face the occasional heart-
pounding hill, you'll enjoy shaded beech woods and
hedgerow-lined bridleways. The Cotswolds, an Area
of Outstanding Natural Beauty, have long attracted
people to their gentle slopes and the Way is drenched
in history from Roman Baths to Tudor manors to
Neolithic long barrows, abbeys, castles and towers.**

Most people walk the way from north to south, if only so
they can spend a day or two exploring the splendour of
Bath at the end of their exertions. Chipping Campden is
a fine introduction to the Cotswolds – a market town of
golden terraces and rose-thronged gardens, of Morris
dancers and historic coaching inns. In more modern times,
Chipping Campden was a centre for the Arts and Crafts
movement, being the home of Ashbee's Guild of Handicraft.

You'll face a steep climb up Dover's Hill as your introduction
to the Cotswold Way – in the 1600s, the hilltop was home
to the Cotswold Olimpick Games, where contestants
participated in shin kicking and tug of war competitions.
On top of Broadway Hill, you'll find Broadway Tower,
designed by Capability Brown and James Wyatt. The
highest tower in the Cotswolds, on a clear day you can see
sixteen counties from the top. In 1661, on the site where
the tower now stands, Joan, John and Richard Perry were
hanged for the murder of William Harrison. Harrison's

bloodied clothes, but not his body, had been found on the
road out of Chipping Campden and the Perrys' admission
to robbery was taken as a confession to murder. A year
after their execution, the very much alive Harrison
suddenly reappeared in Chipping Campden claiming to
have been abducted, placed on board a ship, seized by
Ottoman pirates, sold into slavery and finally escaped and
fled via Portugal. The intricacies of the case that came to be
known as the Campden Wonder have never been solved.

Broadway, with its main street lined with red chestnut
trees, is one of the prettiest Cotswold villages and
a popular first night stop for those wanting a gentle
introduction to the trail. After walking under beech,
elm and sycamore near Winchcombe, you'll pass
Beckbury Camp, an Iron Age fort, and next to it the
Beckbury Monument, said to be the spot where Thomas
Cromwell stood and watched the destruction of Hailes
Abbey during Henry VIII's Dissolution of the Monasteries.
You'll pass the ruins of the thirteenth-century abbey on the
outskirts of Winchcombe.

On the road out of Winchombe, more history awaits you
– Sudeley Castle became the home of Henry VIII's last wife,
Catherine Parr, when she remarried after the King's death.
She is buried there, and reputedly her ghost still haunts the
castle corridors. Next, past generous apple, pear and horse
chestnut trees, there is another notable tomb, Belas Knap,
a Neolithic long barrow.

◄ CROSSING FIELDS TOWARDS NORTH NIBLEY.
© THE WALKING ENGLISHMAN/WWW.WALKINGENGLISHMAN.COM

Postlip Hall looks just like the other manor houses dotted en route, but a pioneering co-housing community was founded here in 1970, and still thrives today. If you want to understand a little of their community ethos, they host the Cotswold Beer Festival in their medieval tithe barn every July.

Cleeve Hill (317 metres) is the highest point on the Cotswold Way, with fine views towards the Brecon Beacons and the Severn Estuary. Above Leckhampton, you'll pass the Devil's Chimney, a tower of limestone, either formed by erosion or quarrying. Or from the stones that the devil used to hurl at local churchgoers.

The Cotswolds lay claim to being the final resting place of another Queen. A Celtic grave discovered near Birdlip in 1879 is said to contain the remains of Boudicca, although there is some evidence that the skeleton interred is male, and many other places lay claim to Boudicca – there is a legend that her remains are buried under Kings Cross railway station in London.

You take an easier route over Cooper's Hill than the cheese rollers. Every May, hundreds of runners sprint, slide and somersault down this northern flank of this hill in pursuit of a large Double Gloucestershire cheese. Painswick Beacon offers another Iron Age fort, and panoramic views into Wales, before you descend to the lowest section of the Way along the Stroudwater Navigation canal.

At Dursley – a name that perhaps inspired J.K. Rowling, who grew up not far from here – you can visit the Old Spot Inn, a pub named for the local pig breed, which has been the recipient of many rewards, including CAMRA National Pub of the Year in 2007. Near North Nibley, you'll climb the steep bridleway to the Tyndale Monument, built to commemorate William Tyndale who first translated the bible into English

LOOKING TOWARDS THE SEVERN VALLEY FROM COALEY PEAK. © ADAM LONG

(and who was executed for his pains). You can climb the 121 steps to the top of the tower for a glimpse of the River Severn.

On the outskirts of Bath, Dyrham Park is famous for its herds of fallow deer. You may curse the trail's creators who decided the Way should meander through the tourist-thronged streets of Bath to the abbey but nothing is quite so telling of the history of the city as this spot, in the triangle between the medieval Bath Abbey, the Regency Pump Room and the Roman Baths.

Summer is the most popular time to walk the Way, but accommodation may be scarce. Far better to visit in spring, when the hedgerows will be fragrant with pink hawthorn blossom, and the woods will reek of the wild garlic under your feet. Under the shade of the trees, you'll find a sea of iridescent bluebells and the villages will dance with daffodils. If you're lucky, you might even discover a wild orchid. The weather will rarely preclude walking the Way, although grassy paths may become very muddy during winter and spring. The route is mainly through farmland, on footpaths, and sometimes bridleways. There are short sections of country road, and many sections of well-established deciduous woods.

Bath has direct railway connections to London and Bristol. The nearest international airports are Bristol, Birmingham and London. Moreton-in-Marsh, with direct connections to London, is the closest railway station to Chipping Campden – there are bus connections from Moreton-in-Marsh to Chipping Campden. Midway, the route passes close to Cheltenham and Gloucester, which both offer good onward rail connections. There is plenty of bed and breakfast accommodation on the route, but very few alternatives – there are no campsites and little opportunity for wild camping.

The Cotswold Way is a gentle trail through England's bucolic countryside. The Cotswolds, long a retreat for London's weary workers, are a world away from Britain's capital city – they offer a return to a gentler way of life. The Cotswold Way is not a walk through Britain's untamed moorland, or a trek through exposed fells, but it does offer a glimpse of the green and pleasant land at the very heart of England.

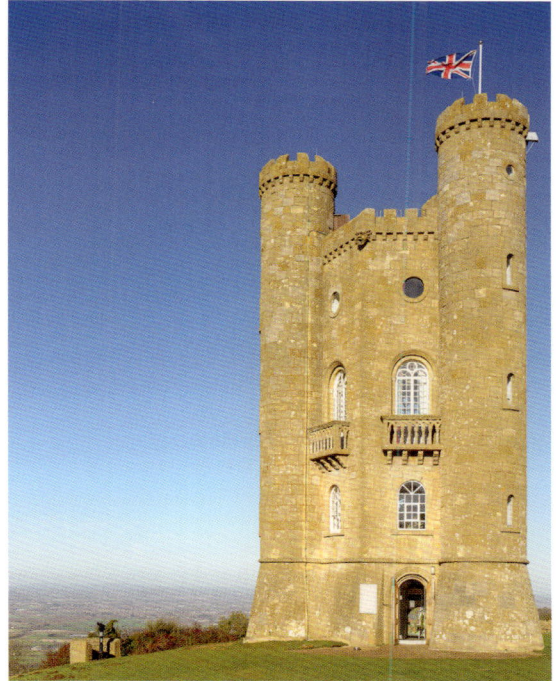

ABOVE: BROADWAY TOWER. © ADAM LONG

BELOW: BARROW WAKE NEAR BIRDLIP. © ADAM LONG

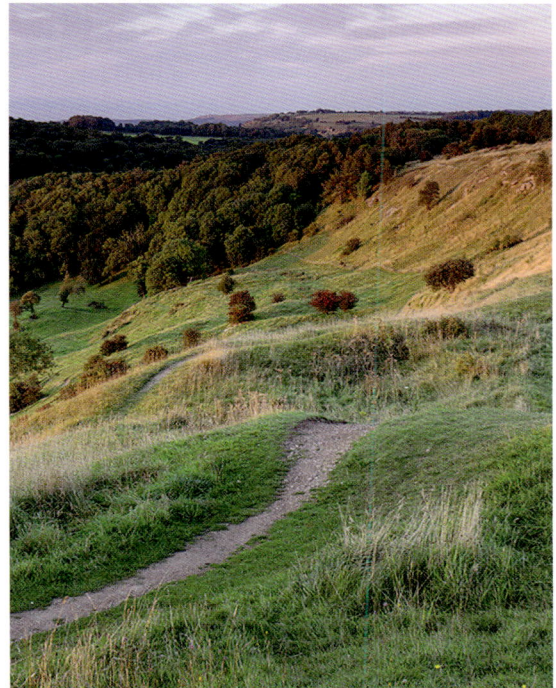

TRAIL ESSENTIALS

Start:	**Chipping Campden, Gloucestershire, England**
End:	**Bath, Somerset, England**
Distance:	**168km**
Ascent/descent:	**3,750m/3,860m**

HOW TO GET THERE

Chipping Campden has bus connections to the closest train station at Moreton-in-Marsh (and Cheltenham) – London is approximately ninety minutes away by rail.

Bath has good rail connections to Bristol and other English cities – Birmingham and London are approximately two hours away. Bristol is the closest international airport.

TIME TO COMPLETE

Walking:	**9 days/51 hours**
Trekking:	**5 days/41 hours**
Fastpacking:	**4 days/31 hours**
Trail running:	**3 days/22 hours**

PROS

- **History** – from the Roman city of Bath to Iron Age hill forts, medieval abbeys and Civil War battle sites, there is plenty for the history buff to discover en route.

- **Villages** – famed for their biscuit-tin prettiness, the golden-stoned Cotswold villages are one of the highlights of the Cotswold Way. Expect flowered gardens, thatched roofs, and a warm welcome in traditional pubs.

- **Bath** – where the Romans built a temple, where Beau Nash held society enthralled, where Jane Austen's ladies came to dance – is one of Britain's prettiest (and sunniest) cities.

CONS

- **Farmland** – this is not a walk across windswept moors or high coast paths, but very much through hedgerow-trimmed pastures and fields of corn.

- **Urban sprawl** – you are never too far from civilisation on the Cotswold Way. On a clear day, you may be able to see the Black Mountains of Wales. On most days, you'll be able to see Cheltenham, Gloucester or Bath.

GOOD TO KNOW

The Cotswold Olimpick Games have been held near Chipping Campden since 1612. Categories contested include morris dancing, tug of war and shin kicking.

FURTHER INFORMATION

www.nationaltrail.co.uk/en_GB/trails/cotswold-way

JAN	FEB	MAR	APR	MAY	JUN	JUL	AUG	SEP	OCT	NOV	DEC

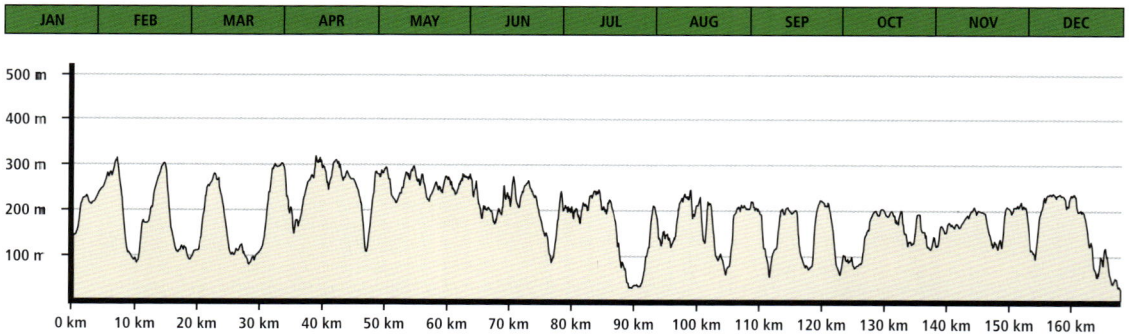

08 DALES WAY
— 127km

When the summer crowds are rushing to the Lake District, the wiser walkers are enjoying the quieter, gentler beauty of the Yorkshire Dales, just the other side of the M6 motorway. The 127-kilometre Dales Way is a gentle path, following rivers, through Yorkshire's green dales, from Ilkley to the southern fringes of the Lake District at Bowness-on-Windermere. This is not a wind-charged challenge, across boggy fells, but rather a bucolic stroll between tearoom-filled-villages — the perfect family holiday.

The Dales Way begins in the pretty spa town of Ilkley, with its Victorian shopping arcade and Bettys Tea Rooms. The Victorians flocked here for the healing spring waters; if in search of aquatic rejuvenation now, you need look no further than the mushroom-shaped lido, with its beautiful Yorkshire Dales backdrop. The start of the Way is at the old bridge over the River Wharfe, and the route follows the course of the river, through Wharfedale, for its first fifty kilometres.

Near the village of Addingham, you'll pass the Farfield Friends Meeting House which, having been built in 1689, is one of the oldest Quaker meeting houses in the world. Another religious wonder, the ruins of Bolton Priory, await you a little further along the river — you may have to queue if you want to cross the river's stepping stones at this tourist hotspot. The river cuts a deep, furious path through a gorge known as the Strid — legend has it that no one who has entered the river here has survived, so you would be well advised to enjoy the oak-lined path rather than risking a swim.

The path follows the river through the pretty Dales villages of Burnsall and Linton, before passing Linton Falls to enter the bustling market town of Grassington — with plenty of tearooms (and a couple of pubs) around the cobbled market square, you may be tempted to linger on a rainy day. The Dales Way takes a low contour, through limestone landscape, around Great Whernside to reach Kettlewell — the youth hostel here doubles as the village post office, and a second-hand bookshop.

Through grassy and often muddy fields, the Way follows the course of the river towards Buckden, and then past pretty cascades to Beckermonds where you finally part company with the River Wharfe. As you leave the river and climb towards the Cam High Road, where the route briefly joins the Pennine Way, you may be grateful for the shelter offered by the Nature Barn at Nethergill Farm, where tea and coffee are available, with an honesty box.

The Roman Cam High Road, which takes you to the highest point on the Dales Way at 521 metres, offers you fine views of Whernside, Pen-y-Ghent and Ingleborough — the Yorkshire Three Peaks. The route here crosses the Pennine watershed, the line that divides east from west, and decides which rivers flow to the eastern North Sea and which to the western Irish Sea. The traditional route leaves the Pennine Way to head for the cluster of houses at Gearstones, but some choose instead to take the new Pennine Bridleway, opened in 2012, towards Dent — this alternative results in less road walking.

◀ WAYMARKER BY THE RIVER WHARFE BETWEEN STARBOTTON AND KETTLEWELL.
© STEPHEN ROSS

LOOKING UP THE RIVER KENT TOWARDS THE HOWGILLS. © STEPHEN ROSS

The traditional route passes under the Settle–Carlisle Railway, England's most scenic line, at Dent Head Viaduct – you will have enjoyed views of the more famous Ribblehead Viaduct from the Cam High Road. Although still in the West Riding of Yorkshire, you have now crossed into Cumbria, thanks to local government reorganisations of 1974. After a return to riverside walking through Dentdale, the Dales Way follows the River Rawthey at the pretty hamlet of Millthrop, skirting around Sedbergh, but it's worth a detour to take in the town's famous bookshops.

There is no longer a pub at the deceptively named Lincoln's Inn Bridge, and the iron-bridged Waterside Viaduct, another viaduct for the disused Lune Valley Railway, now carries a gas pipe into Sedbergh. You cross the lower, medieval stone-arched Crook of Lune Bridge, which marks your departure from the Yorkshire Dales National Park – before passing under a second viaduct, the now disused, eleven-arched Lowgill Viaduct.

The M6 motorway and a busy railway line must be crossed to reach the next national park, the Lake District National Park. Another river, the River Kent, is your route through the village of Burneside and then into the Lake District. While the high peaks provide a distant backdrop to your walk, this southern part of the Lakes is gentler territory, and the riverside route to Staveley is flat.

The Dales Way leaves the River Kent just before Staveley, turning westwards on the outskirts of the town, but it's a short detour to Staveley Mill Yard, which houses the glass-fronted Beer Hall, the brewery tap for the neighbouring Hawkshead Brewery. Staveley Mill Yard is home to a number of other independent food shops and cafes, as well as Wheelbase, the UK's largest cycle store, and the headquarters of Inov-8, the outdoor running specialists. Wheelbase organises a number of cycling sportives every year, including the seventy-eight-kilometre Tour de Staveley in July.

After Staveley, the Dales Way offers fine views of the distant Old Man of Coniston as it gently crosses undulating farmland and over the sheep-strewn Fell Plain to reach its finishing point at Bowness-on-Windermere. The building of the railway to nearby Windermere brought tourists to this popular lakeside town. Bowness is home to The World

WALLED TRACK BETWEEN BUCKDEN AND STARBOTTON. © STEPHEN ROSS

of Beatrix Potter attraction – the author's farmhouse Hill Top is just across the lake, near Hawkshead (where the Hawkshead Brewery was founded in 2002, before it moved to its larger premises at Staveley). You can catch a ferry across Windermere, England's largest natural lake, to visit the farmhouse, now looked after by the National Trust.

The low-level paths of the Dales Way mean that it can be walked at any time of year, although snow may make navigation more challenging. The route is largely on grassy paths and sometimes trails, although there are short road sections. The route is waymarked, and generally straight-forward to navigate. There are plenty of bed and breakfasts, bunkhouses and hostels en route, accustomed to looking after weary walkers. Although there are few campsites on the route, local farmers are often amenable to allowing wild camping, sometimes for a small fee. Dogs are welcome on the Dales Way although, as the route passes through large swathes of farmland, care should be taken to ensure they are on a lead around livestock, particularly during the spring lambing season.

Ilkley has good rail connections to nearby Leeds and Bradford, and has a direct bus link to Leeds Bradford airport. Bowness-on-Windermere is approximately two kilometres from the railway station in nearby Windermere – buses connect the two neighbours. Connections may be made to the West Coast Main Line at Oxenholme – trains on the West Coast Main Line link London to Glasgow via Manchester, which has an international airport.

The Dales Way celebrated its fiftieth birthday in 2019, and it is one of Britain's most beloved long-distance trails. The Way offers gentle days of grassy paths, with some of Britain's most spectacular scenery as the backdrop. You'll find yourself with plenty of time to picnic by shaded rivers, to admire the hilly views, and to explore the pretty villages en route. Or to warm yourself in another cosy tearoom, sharing trail tales with fellow walkers, as you wait for the rains to pass.

TRAIL ESSENTIALS

Start:	**Ilkley, West Yorkshire, England**
End:	**Bowness-on-Windermere, Cumbria, England**
Distance:	**127km**
Ascent/descent:	**1,570m/1,600m**

HOW TO GET THERE

Ilkley has a train station, offering services to Leeds and Bradford, where connections can be made to other British cities. There is also a direct bus service between Leeds Bradford Airport and Ilkley.

Bowness-on-Windermere has bus connections to Windermere, which offers local train services. Connections with mainline services can be made at Oxenholme. The closest international airport is at Manchester.

TIME TO COMPLETE

Walking:	**6 days/33 hours**
Trekking:	**4 days/27 hours**
Fastpacking:	**3 days/20 hours**
Trail running:	**2 days/15 hours**

PROS

• **Tearooms** – Bettys is a Yorkshire institution, serving Taylors Yorkshire Tea and fruity fat rascals. There are only six Bettys Tea Rooms, all in Yorkshire, one in Ilkley. There are plenty of other tearooms to be found en route.

• **Great for novices** – this is an easy route, taking a low line, through many towns and villages. Volunteers work hard to maintain the trail and to ensure that it is well waymarked, and local businesses and accommodation providers are used to welcoming weary walkers. It is a great route for those who want to try fastpacking or trail running a long-distance trail.

• **Bookshops** – Sedbergh is England's official Book Town, with numerous booksellers, for both new and second-hand books, and a busy calendar of literary events and workshops.

CONS

• **Tantalising views** – the Dales Way offers great views of the Yorkshire Three Peaks and the mountain tops of the Lake District, but no opportunity to summit them. This is not a route for mountain goats.

• **Terrain** – while there are grassy paths through farmland to enjoy, much of this route is on tarmacked paths and there are some road sections.

GOOD TO KNOW

The fastest known time of twelve hours and forty-four minutes was set in 1989 by Dennis Beresford – he set the first fastest known time for completion in the early 1980s, but had to reclaim his record. To celebrate the fiftieth birthday of the Dales Way in 2019, an ultramarathon was run over the route. The very first walkers were somewhat slower – a group of Venture Scouts from Bradford were the first people to walk the entire route, over three and a half days in April 1969.

FURTHER INFORMATION

www.dalesway.org

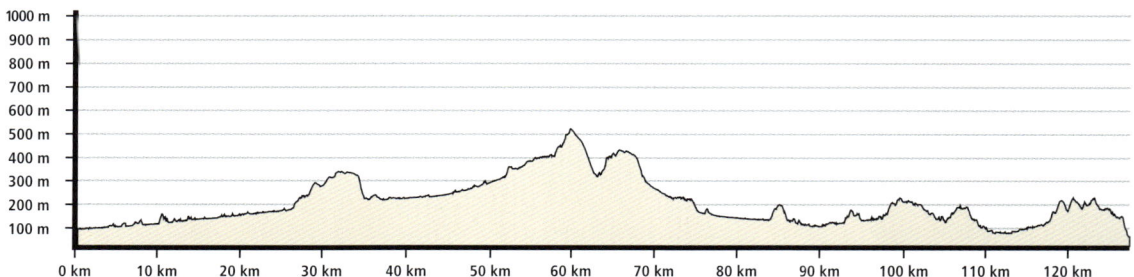

JAN	FEB	MAR	APR	MAY	JUN	JUL	AUG	SEP	OCT	NOV	DEC

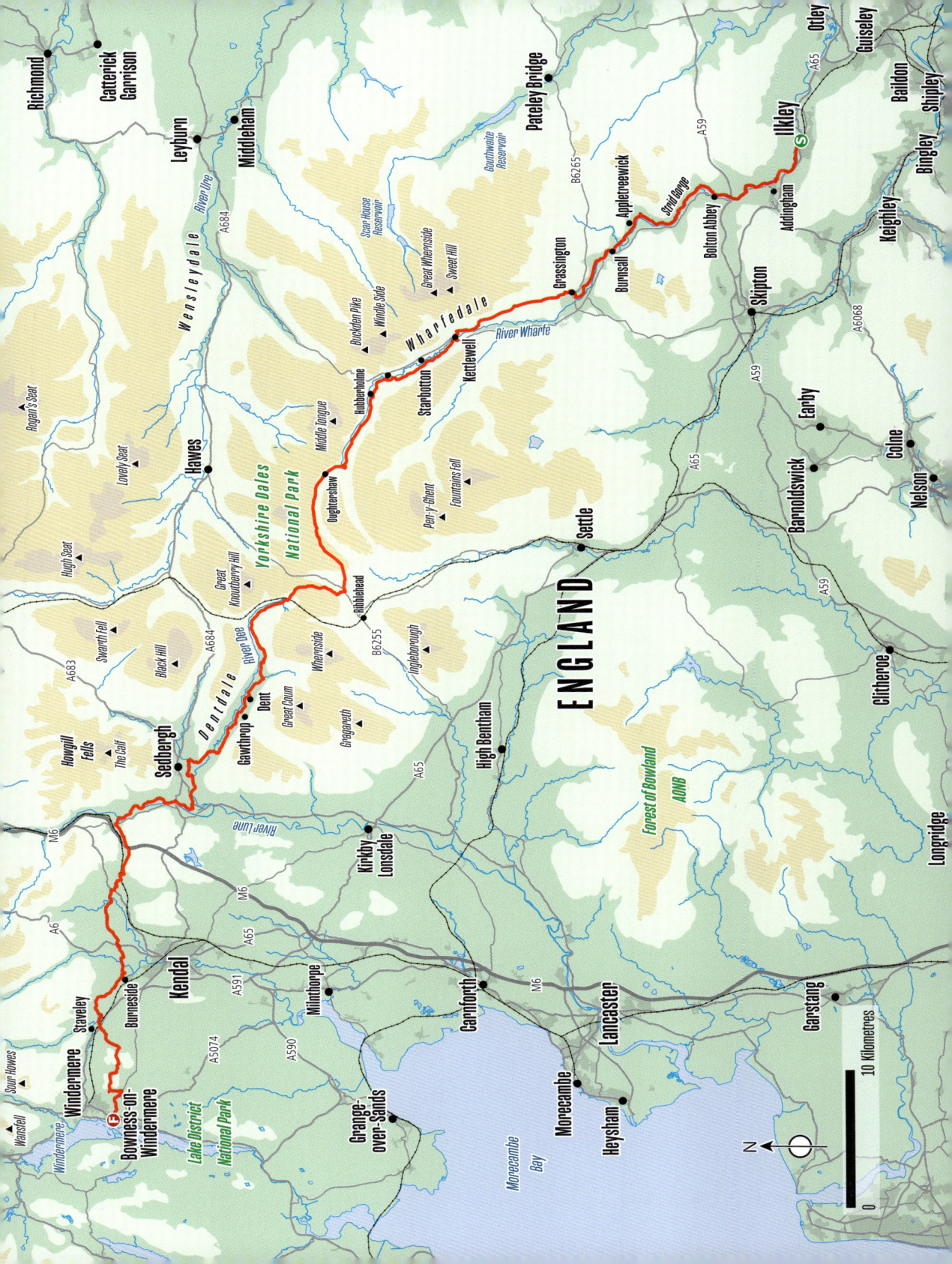

09 HADRIAN'S WALL PATH
– 138km

Once Hadrian's Wall marked the edge of the world, the northern boundary of the Roman Empire. The Romans built this stone defence on the dolerite cliffs of Great Whin Sill for its high vantage point and sweeping views. Though the milehouses have crumbled, and the garrisons fallen silent, the 138-kilometre Hadrian's Wall Path still offers panoramic views of forest and grey-green moors, the peaks of the distant Lake District and the sea-lapped shores of the Solway Firth.

Hadrian's Wall Path, the only National Trail to cross England coast to coast (almost!), can be walked in either direction. Walking from west to east means that you'll have the wind pushing you forward, rather than driving rain in your face. It also gives you a gentle start to your journey, along the flat Solway Firth. But, in the other direction, the vibrant city of Newcastle upon Tyne, with its cheerful pubs and multitude of restaurants, is an excellent precursor to any walk. If you want to shorten your first long day and arrive early enough the day before, you might choose to catch the Metro to Wallsend, where the Roman fort Segedunum marks the start of the trail. You can explore the small museum at the fort, and buy a Hadrian's Wall Passport to be stamped en route, before walking eight kilometres back to the centre of Newcastle.

The route follows a disused railway line, before reaching the banks of the Tyne – this graffitied and littered section is not the best introduction to a National Trail, but the vista of Newcastle, and Gateshead, is impressive as are the seven bridges across the Tyne. The two-tiered High Level Bridge still carries trains above the heads of pedestrians and car drivers over the river. The soaring arches of the Tyne Bridge were designed by Mott, Hay and Anderson, who also designed the Sydney Harbour Bridge and Forth Road Bridge.

It takes a while to leave the sprawl of Newcastle behind, though the paths through parks and along the river are pleasant enough. You will encounter signs for Hadrian's Cycleway, a coast to coast cycling route that sometimes coincides with Hadrian's Wall Path. Part of this shared bridleway follows the Wylam Waggonway – used to transport coal from Wylam Colliery to the Tyne, this was one of Britain's first railways. The trucks, on wooden rails, were originally pulled by horses but in 1815, a young local apprentice, George Stephenson, watched as William Hedley built a prototype steam engine, the *Puffing Billy*.

At Heddon-on-the-Wall, you'll glimpse your first proper view of the Wall, and the Vallum earthworks ditch in front of it. However, for the next twenty kilometres, the more dominant historical feature is the Military Road, built in 1754, to facilitate troop movement after the Jacobite Rebellion – it's now the lorry-heavy B6318.

The first extant stone section of the Wall is encountered at Planetrees. If you only have a couple of days to explore Hadrian's Wall Path, this section between Chollerford and Birdoswald is the most history-rich, picturesque part of the trail. This beautiful wall-topped ridge traverses up and down between milecastles and forts.

◄ CUDDY'S CRAGS PROVIDE GOOD VIEWS ALONG THE EASTERN PART OF THE CENTRAL SECTION OF HADRIAN'S WALL.
© ROGER CLEGG/WWW.HADRIANSWALLGALLERY.COM

On the outskirts of Chollerford, you can visit the Chesters Roman Fort (and museum). Brocolitia, once privately owned but gifted to the nation in 2020, is home not only to a fort but also a Temple of Mithras.

Near Milecastle 35, Sewing Shields Farm is one of the local buildings constructed (in the nineteenth century) from the stones of the wall. At Housesteads Roman Fort, you can admire the wonders of Roman plumbing – the latrines are the best-preserved part of the fort. At Cuddy's Crags, the Pennine Way joins Hadrian's Wall. This switchback section of the wall involves knee-jarring ups and downs, sometimes over stone steps.

At Steel Rigg, you are approaching the halfway point of the wall. The solitary tree standing in the dipped curve of Sycamore Gap is perhaps the most famous view on the trail. The fort of Vindolanda, just off the trail, predates the Wall. At Once Brewed, the Twice Brewed Inn used to sit next to a basic youth hostel but, in 2017, the YHA opened a brand new, eco-friendly hostel and National Landscape Discovery Centre here.

Green Slack (345 metres) on Winshields Crags is the highest point on the way. The Wall begins to fade from view although Walltown Crags offers one final splendid section of turrets and wall. At the old quarry, now a country park, you'll find toilets and a bus stop in the car park and, close by, the Roman Army Museum.

Near the village of Greenhead, a popular overnight stop, you'll pass the ruins of the twelfth-century Thirlwall Castle, another building constructed from the Wall's stones. The village of Gilsland, on the River Irthing, is half Northumbrian, half Cumbrian; it straddles the counties' borders. At Birdoswald Roman Fort, the best preserved fort en route, you have a rare opportunity to see the stone wall running parallel to the older turf wall structure. West of Birdoswald, it is this turf wall that guides the path, a ridge and dip through the fields.

ABOVE: BETWEEN SEWING SHIELDS CRAGS AND KENNEL CRAGS. © ROGER CLEGG

BELOW: SYCAMORE GAP ON MIDSUMMER'S NIGHT. © ROGER CLEGG

STEEL RIGG AND PEEL CRAGS ON AN EXHILARATING LATE WINTER MORNING WITH CRAG LOUGH RECEDING INTO THE BANK OF FOG.
© ROGER CLEGG/WWW.HADRIANSWALLGALLERY.COM

The route leaves the high, wild Sill behind to pass through farmland and dappled woods, occasionally meandering through quiet villages. Under an arched avenue of trees, you pass Carlisle's small airport and at Crosby-on-Eden you join the river. The River Eden leads you into the historic city of Carlisle.

To all but the most acute archaeological eye, the wall disappears completely after Carlisle. The trail follows the River Eden, occasionally cutting away through green meadows, to where the river merges with the Solway Firth. Somewhere on these flat, wide marshes, near Burgh by Sands, Edward I, the Hammer of the Scots, died. The trail along the firth, often on tediously flat roads, does at least reward you with fine views of the Scottish Lowlands and the Lakeland peaks, at their front, Skiddaw. A short section, near Drumburgh, can flood at particularly high tides – you should check with local tourist information before embarking on it.

The route ends in the small village of Bowness-on-Solway. There is little to distract you here other than one pub and two tearooms, but only two or three buses a day run back towards Carlisle. For this reason, some choose to walk this last section from Bowness to Carlisle rather than face an expensive taxi journey. Only the worst weather of winter would prevent you from walking the Hadrian's Wall Path, but you are encouraged to walk it between May and October for conservation reasons. Buses may be infrequent and accommodation closed out of season.

Hadrian's Wall Path is often suggested as a good path for beginners, and for many it begins a lifetime's love affair with long-distance trails. Rich with history, offering stunning views, this trail across a country's width is beautiful but not as easy as it seems. Though there are tearooms, pubs, and farms en route, they are widely spaced. You will often face kilometres over exposed moorland. This is not a trail that will capture your heart from the very start, but it reveals its true beauty when you reach the Wall, and see the grey line stretch far across the bronzed moorland in front of you.

09 HADRIAN'S WALL PATH: ESSENTIAL INFORMATION

TRAIL ESSENTIALS

Start:	**Wallsend, North Tyneside, England**
End:	**Bowness-on-Solway, Cumbria, England**
Distance:	**138km**
Ascent/descent:	**1,330m/1,340m**

HOW TO GET THERE

Wallsend is on the Tyne and Wear Metro, with a direct connection to Newcastle's central stations. Newcastle International Airport is also served by the Metro, and Newcastle offers high-speed rail links to other English and Scottish cities.

Bowness-on-Solway is poorly served by public transport, with only two or three buses each day (returning to Carlisle). Carlisle has a small airport, and has high-speed rail connections to other cities (and a direct service back to Newcastle).

TIME TO COMPLETE

Walking:	**6 days/35 hours**
Trekking:	**4 days/28 hours**
Fastpacking:	**3 days/21 hours**
Trail running:	**2 days/16 hours**

PROS

• **History** – the route does not only offer the Wall and the 300 centuries of Roman occupation. The ancient city of Carlisle also contains plenty of historical sites, having been an important strategic military stronghold – Mary, Queen of Scots, was once held prisoner there.

• **Great for beginners** – Hadrian's Wall Path isn't easy – there are plenty of ups and downs, and sometimes limited facilities. But it's well waymarked, and you're never too far from a road – in summer, a bus passes regularly back and forth along the Military Road, making it easy to break your days. Plenty of companies offer supported holidays and baggage transfers along the route.

• **Coast to coast** – to truly walk coast to coast, some walkers choose to start at Tynemouth, approximately seven kilometres east of Wallsend. Although Wainwright's popular route suggests a challenging coast to coast path across England, Hadrian's Wall Path is the only National Trail to offer a (waymarked) traverse across England, from the North Sea to the Irish Sea.

CONS

• **Popular** – Hadrian's Wall Path is one Britain's most popular long-distance trails. The Wall attracts more than 100,000 visitors a year, so hotspots such as Housesteads Roman Fort may be busy, particularly in July and August.

• **Military Road** – the early sections of the trail follow the Military Road, now a busy road.

• **Accommodation** – there is limited accommodation en route. Fortunately, the AD122 bus provides a convenient link to larger towns such as Hexham and Haltwhistle, (with connections on to Carlisle or Newcastle).

GOOD TO KNOW

In April 2016, Kendal resident Jacob Snochowski set the record for running the trail (sixteen hours and twenty-five minutes), breaking the previous record by three hours. Polish-born Snochowski, who had only been a runner for three years, was raising money for Cumbrians affected by the devastation of Storm Desmond in December 2015.

FURTHER INFORMATION

www.nationaltrail.co.uk/en_GB/trails/hadrians-wall-path;
Hadrian's Wall Path Guidemap (Vertebrate Publishing, 2020).

JAN	FEB	MAR	APR	MAY	JUN	JUL	AUG	SEP	OCT	NOV	DEC

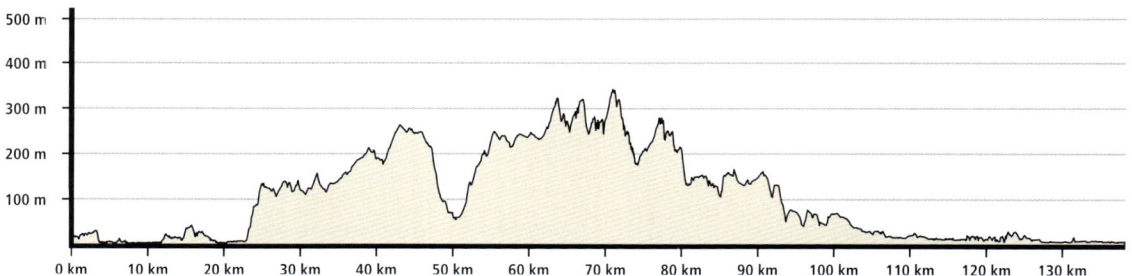

Amble

Blyth

South
Shields

Newton Aycliffe

Morpeth

Cramlington

Wallsend **S** Segedunum (Roman fort)

Washington

A1(M)

Spennymoor

Shildon

Ponteland

Belsay

Newcastle-upon Tyne

Gateshead

Ryton

Whickham

Stanley

Durham

Bishop Auckland

Heddon-on-the-Wall

Prudhoe

Consett

A68

A696

Corbridge

Derwent Reservoir

A697

A1

A1068

A69

Hexham

A686

River North Tyne

Chollerford

Planetrees

Chesters (Roman fort)

Brocolitia (Roman fort)

Newbrough

A689

West Woodburn

A68

Housesteads (Roman fort)

Vindolanda (Roman fort)

Bardon Mill

River South Tyne

Alston

Rochester

Byrness

Northumberland National Park

Green Slack

Once Brewed

Haltwhistle

North Pennines AONB

Falstone

Haydon

Kielder Water

Gilsland

Greenhead

Lambley

The Pennines

Kielder

ENGLAND

Birdoswald (Roman fort)

A69

River Irthing

Brampton

River Eden

Penrith

A66

Walton

Cheviot Hills

SCOTLAND

Longtown

M6

A595

A7

River Esk

Carlisle

River Eden

Wigton

Lake District National Park

Langholm

Beaumont

Gretna

Drumburgh

Burgh-by-Sands

Annan

Bowness-on-Solway **F**

A74(M)

River Annan

20 Kilometres

0

N

10 ICKNIELD WAY PATH – 182km

CAMBRIDGE

St Albans

Edward Thomas, the war poet, loved England's old roads, and thought nothing of rising at dawn to walk fifty kilometres in a day. In 1913, he published an account of his ten-day hike along one of Britain's oldest roads, the Icknield Way. The 182-kilometre Icknield Way Path, from Ivinghoe Beacon to Knettishall Heath follows in his footsteps, and is one link of the Greater Ridgeway, a trail across England from Dorset to Norfolk. These paths, trodden through the grass long before the Romans arrived, follow a chalk ridge, past the ruins of Neolithic settlements, Roman battlefields and medieval villages. Today, the Icknield Way Path is a more peaceful place, a haven for lapwings and skylarks, badgers and dormice.

The Icknield Way Path begins where the Ridgeway (another section of the Greater Ridgeway) ends, on Ivinghoe Beacon, a hill topped by an Iron Age fort in Buckinghamshire. Butterflies flock to the flowered slopes of the Chilterns, where you might find rare orchids and pasque flowers. On the border of Buckinghamshire and Bedfordshire, the Way skirts around Whipsnade Zoo, affording you glimpses of bison and wallabies. You may already have seen the Whipsnade White Lion carved into the hillside; it was commissioned in 1933 by the zoo to warn pilots not to scare the animals by flying too low.

Seeing the evening light glow through a copse of trees, Edmond Blyth conceived a memorial to his friends, and all the others, killed during World War I. The Icknield Way Path passes Blyth's Whipsnade Tree Cathedral, the walls of which are of beech, ash and oak. Dunstable Downs is

the highest area of Bedfordshire, offering views over five counties, and of the gliders from the London Gliding Club. The Way passes Five Knolls, where there are seven Neolithic burial mounds, and then crosses the ancient Watling Street.

The route leaves the beautiful Chilterns to traverse a flatter, more urban landscape, as it passes the outskirts of Luton and crosses the M1. You can choose a variation into Toddington, a village with six pubs. After Sundon Hills Country Park, the Way makes a brief return to the final edges of the Chilterns. After passing the Iron Age boundary earthworks of Drays Ditches, the route climbs Telegraph Hill – this was named after the semaphore signalling station, part of a network built during the Napoleonic Wars.

Although Letchworth is now known as the first Garden City, Ebenezer Howard's vision of urban living combined with the benefits of the country, Letchworth was recorded as a settlement as early as the Domesday Book. Among the innovations created for the Garden City, Letchworth is home to the UK's first roundabout. The Way through Hertfordshire leaves behind the urban sprawl to follow grassy paths between pretty hamlets. One rural village, Wallington, was home to the newly-married writer George Orwell, who ran the village shop.

There are more (Bronze Age) barrows on the high Therfield Heath, just above Royston – an ancient settlement that stood at the crossroads of Ermine Street and the Icknield Way, and was once home to a royal hunting lodge.

◀ WOOD LANE, A GREENWAY SOUTH-WEST OF PIRTON IN NORTH HERTFORDSHIRE. © CHRISTINE JAMES

In 1742, a cave, its wall elaborately carved with religious symbolry, was discovered under the town's crossroads – no one knows who dug the beehive-shaped hollow out from the chalk, or what it was used for, although some link it to Freemasonry. The cave, which the route passes over, is open to the public.

In Cambridgeshire, the Way follows the wooded remains of Bran Ditch, earthworks thought to be Anglo-Saxon. Excavations in the 1920s discovered more than fifty headless skeletons, believed to be Saxon warriors. After its brief foray into Cambridgeshire, the route enters Essex and the Icknield villages, agricultural settlements that later become outposts of Saffron Walden's wool industry. In one of these villages, Great Chesterford, there is another subterranean mystery – a secret tunnel, some traces of which have been uncovered, was said to connect the Crown House Hotel to the church and vicarage. The church's silver

bells were hidden there to save them from Roundheads during the Civil War, but they have never been found.

The route enters its sixth and final county, Suffolk, as it traverses field upon field of barley, around the horse racing town of Newmarket. You are now entering the lands of the Iceni, the tribe associated with the warrior queen Boudicca – Icklingham is named for this Celtic tribe. Now it is more chocolate-box villages of thatched cottages. Although kings and queens have long visited, the King's Forest is named for a more modern monarch – it commemorates the silver jubilee of George V and Mary in 1935. This quiet woodland is flower rich with wild thyme and bird's-foot trefoil.

Euston Hall, the ancestral home of the Dukes of Grafton, lends its name to the London railway station; the family owned the land that the station was built on. Elizabeth I

WHIPSNADE TREE CATHEDRAL, CREATED BY EDMOND BLYTH. © SHUTTERSTOCK/STEPHEN BARNES

IVINGHOE BEACON, WHERE THE ICKNIELD WAY PATH CONTINUES FROM THE RIDGEWAY. © SHUTTERSTOCK/JOE DUNCKLEY

once stayed at Euston Hall, and the grounds were landscaped by Capability Brown. It is open to the public and hosts a tearoom, that may offer welcome respite to the walker or runner as there are few other facilities in the area. It is a short, pleasant heathland walk to the end of the trail.

The Icknield Way Path ends inauspiciously in a car park, although there is a variation that takes you to the nearby market town of Thetford. Most who walk the Icknield Way Path undertake it as part of the Greater Ridgeway – the Icknield Way Path begins at the end of the Ridgeway, and it ends where the Peddars Way begins. Although the Way often takes a route over the highest part of the landscape, this is not a route of ascent and descent but rather a gentle path through pastoral terrain. The route's highest point is at its start and it descends towards Suffolk.

This is a quiet route, undiscovered and not often walked. You may struggle to find accommodation – there are bed and breakfasts, small hotels, and village pubs but you may sometimes have to leave the route at the end of the day to find somewhere to stay. Those who camp may find

themselves forced to wild camp on more than one occasion, as there are very few campsites near the route.

The Icknield Way Path may be walked at any time of year, weather permitting, and is not exposed or remote. The route is waymarked with signposts bearing a flint axe, although there are also cycle and horse riding variations of the Way, so care should be taken to ensure you follow the pedestrian route.

On the eve of the World War I, Robert Frost, a close friend of Edward Thomas, would visit him in the Gloucestershire countryside, and they would walk the old ways together. Frost wrote 'The Road Not Taken', that tells of choosing the road less travelled, for Thomas. The Icknield Way was once busy with traders, and soldiers, and pilgrims and now lies quiet. This is a trail for those who love solitude, for those who want to walk through the fields and farms, and see the traces of all those who were there before us.

10 ICKNIELD WAY PATH: ESSENTIAL INFORMATION

TRAIL ESSENTIALS

Start:	**Ivinghoe Beacon, Buckinghamshire, England**
End:	**Knettishall Heath, Suffolk, England**
Distance:	**182km**
Ascent/descent:	**1,560m/1,760m**

HOW TO GET THERE

Ivinghoe Beacon is approximately five kilometres from Tring, where direct rail connections are available to London. Bus services run from Tring to the bottom of the Beacon, but many choose to follow the Ridgeway from Tring instead – the same bus also serves Dunstable, which offers onward connections to London Luton Airport.

Knettishall Heath is served by buses from Thetford, where rail connections to London, generally via Cambridge, can be made. In addition to London's airports, international connections can be made to Rotterdam and Amsterdam via the ferry port at Harwich.

TIME TO COMPLETE

Walking:	**7 days/44 hours**
Trekking:	**5 days/36 hours**
Fastpacking:	**4 days/27 hours**
Trail running:	**3 days/21 hours**

PROS

• **History** – the route is rich in history, from its royal visitors to Saxon defences to medieval mysteries. The path passes Iron Age barrows, Anglo-Saxon earthworks and medieval churches.

• **Undiscovered** – the Icknield Way Path is not a well-known or frequently walked route, and you will often find yourself alone along on the trail. This undisturbed path is frequented by birds, particularly skylarks and stone curlews.

• **Greater Ridgeway** – the Icknield Way Path is one of four routes (the others are the Wessex Ridgeway, the Ridgeway and the Peddars Way) that together form the Greater Ridgeway, a long route across southern England, from Lyme Regis, on the Dorset–Devon border, to Hunstanton on the North Norfolk Coast.

CONS

• **Luton** – the route passes the outskirts of Dunstable and Luton, an unpleasant urban section, that offers lorry parks, industrial estates and shopping centres.

• **Motorways** – the Icknield Way Path crosses three busy motorways (the M1, A1(M) and the M11). The distant hum of motorway traffic is the soundtrack to some sections of the route.

GOOD TO KNOW

The Icknield Way, which extends further than the Icknield Way Path across the Greater Ridgeway, is one of the oldest roads in Britain. It was one of the four medieval highways, believed to have been constructed by royal decree, on which travellers enjoyed royal protection – attacks against travellers on the road were treated as an offence against the King himself.

FURTHER INFORMATION

www.icknieldwaypath.co.uk

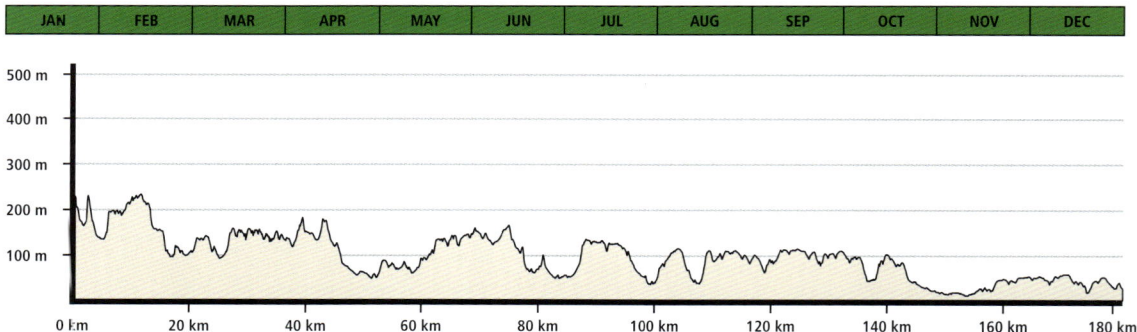

JAN	FEB	MAR	APR	MAY	JUN	JUL	AUG	SEP	OCT	NOV	DEC

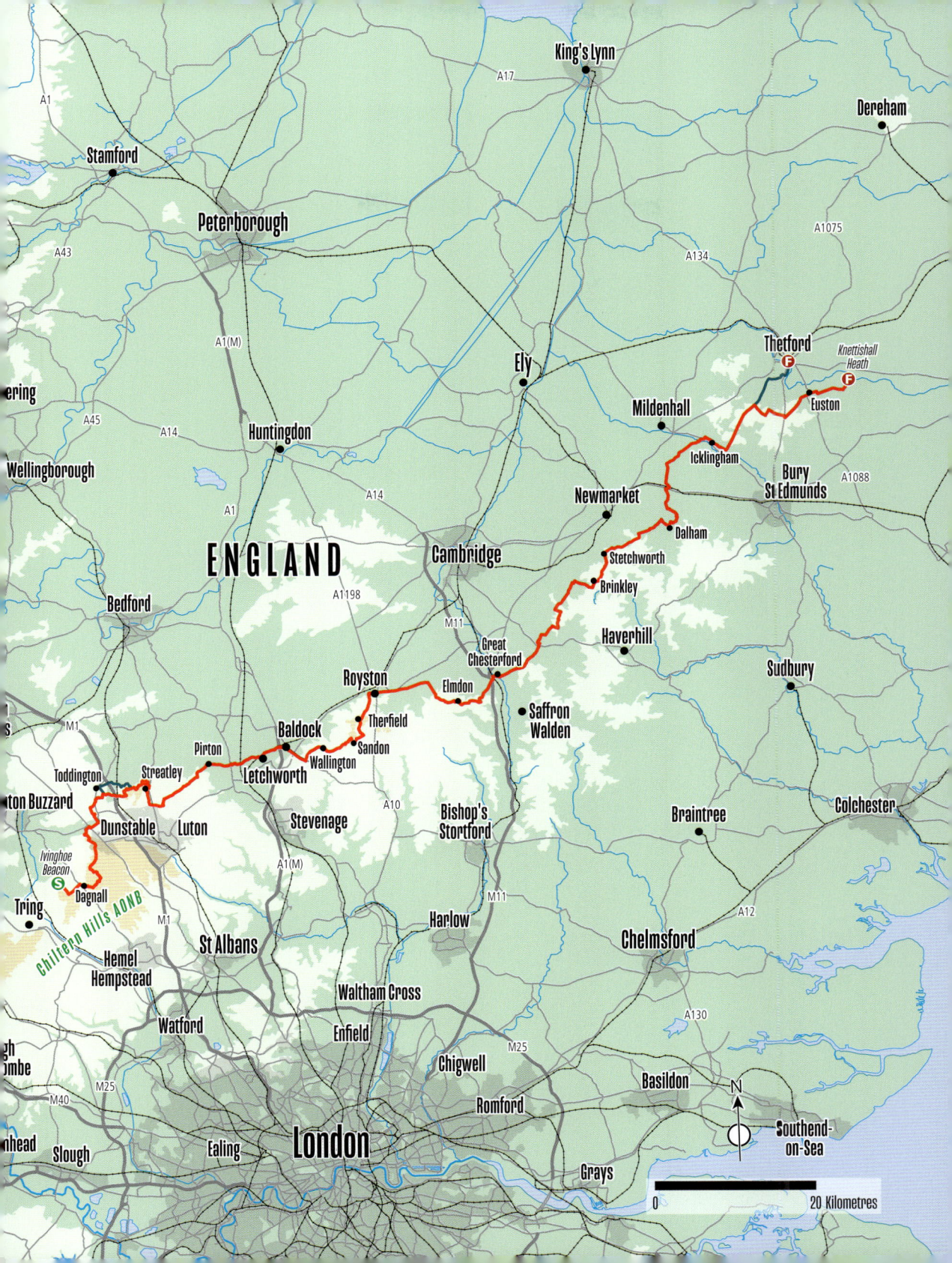

King's Lynn

Dereham

Stamford

Peterborough

A17

A1075

A1(M)

A43

A134

Thetford

Knettishall Heath

Ely

Mildenhall

Euston

ering

A45

A14

Huntingdon

Newmarket

Icklingham

Bury St Edmunds

A1088

Wellingborough

A1

A14

A1198

Dalham

Stetchworth

Brinkley

ENGLAND

Cambridge

Haverhill

Sudbury

Bedford

M11

Great Chesterford

Elmdon

Royston

Saffron Walden

Colchester

M1

Therfield

Baldock

Sandon

Wallington

Letchworth

Pirton

Streatley

Toddington

ton Buzzard

Braintree

A10

Stevenage

Bishop's Stortford

M11

Dunstable

Luton

A1(M)

Ivinghoe Beacon

Dagnall

Chiltern Hills AONB

Tring

Hemel Hempstead

St Albans

Harlow

Chelmsford

A12

Watford

Waltham Cross

M25

A130

Enfield

Chigwell

Basildon

N

gh

ombe

M40

M1

Romford

M25

Grays

Southend-on-Sea

head

Slough

Ealing

London

0   20 Kilometres

11 ISLE OF ANGLESEY COASTAL PATH – 201km

Bangor

Anglesey sits at the very edge of Wales, an island disappearing into the sea. Its low coasts offer golden beaches, rugged cliffs and tiny islands. This is a landscape steeped in myths, where place names tell a story. The 201-kilometre Isle of Anglesey Coastal Path encircles the whole island, rarely leaving the sea. This beautiful path, one of the finest sections of the Wales Coast Path, has something to offer everyone – stunning views, historic sites, and great food.

The official starting point is the medieval St Cybi's Church in Holyhead. The route has an unpromising beginning as it passes the sprawling ferry port and heads for the stark white chimney of the obsolete Anglesey Aluminium works. You'll soon be in the greener, wooded grounds of Penrhos Coastal Park. At the end of Beddmanarch Bay, you can watch the sea gushing through Stanley Embankment, the groundbreaking engineering feat built by Thomas Telford in 1822 to carry the London road to the port of Holyhead.

After you've crossed the Embankment – one of the toll houses is now a tearoom – the beach section at Llanfachraeth is one of several sections of the route that is only passable when the tide is not too high. The new pedestrian bridge over the Afon Alaw, decorated with shields depicting wildlife and legendary figures, saves walkers a tedious detour, kilometres inland, to cross the river.

After putting Penryhn's caravan parks behind you, at Porth Trefadog the coastal scenery becomes wilder. The cliffs rise higher, and the beaches are stony. The sea stacks at

Ynys y Fydlyn are cut off at high tide, but can be reached with care at low tide. At the north-west corner of Anglesey the three painted columns of the White Ladies at Carmel Head, two on the mainland and one on the isle of West Mouse, warn sailors of the dangerous Coal Rock. The other view from this headland is that of the decommissioned Wylfa Nuclear Power Station.

From these deadly seas, one stormy night at Hen Borth in the 1740s, two children, who spoke no English, were rescued from a foundering ship. Adopted by the local doctor, one of them, Evan Thomas, displayed prodigious skills in bonesetting. Generation after generation, the Anglesey bonesetters were famous – Evan's great-grandson invented the Thomas splint, an innovation that reduced deaths from femoral fractures from eighty per cent to eight per cent during World War I.

At Cemlyn Bay, you'll pass the high walls of Vivian Hewitt's house. The fiercely private Hewitt, who in 1912 became the first aviator to fly across the Irish Sea, set up the lagoon here as a bird sanctuary. You can make the strenuous walk across the shingle ridge, or follow the road around the bay. The rocks near Cemaes, a fishing port and holiday destination, are fascinating to geologists as they are a confusing jumble of quartzite, limestone and phyllite.

◀ LOOKING TOWARDS SOUTH STACK LIGHTHOUSE.
© ADAM LONG

At Bull Bay, you may spot dolphins or porpoises, and sometimes even whales. The shoreline, however, bears witness to Anglesey's industrial past – from the disused quarry, to the red towers of the Victorian Porth Wen Brickworks, to Amlwch's Octel bromine works, which are now crumbling despite them only being closed in 2004. The copper mines at Parys Mountain, now a museum, once produced more copper than any other mine in the world.

At Porth Eilian, you turn the north-east corner of the coast – although you might want to detour to the lighthouse. This is another dangerous section of coast – it was at Moelfre that the *Royal Charter*, a steam clipper returning to Liverpool from Australia, foundered in 1859. Approximately 450 passengers died, and a memorial stands to the ship on the coastal path.

The route climbs over the cliffs along wooded paths to Benllech but, at low tide, you can then follow the beach across Red Wharf Bay. At Penmon Point, you can look across the sea to Puffin Island. A twelfth-century monastery once stood on this small island, but now it is a haven for seabirds, although thousands more cormorants nest here than puffins. If you are lucky, you may glimpse seals or dolphins in the choppy waters.

Penmon marks the entrance to the Menai Strait, the narrow stretch of water that separates Anglesey from the Welsh mainland. Beaumaris, once the county town, now a foodie destination, is home to Edward I's most ambitious castle, although it remains unfinished. Before Thomas Telford designed the Menai Suspension Bridge there was no connection to the mainland, and farmers wishing to sell their cattle would have to drive them into the water and force them to swim across the Menai Strait. The Coastal Path passes underneath the bridge, and along the Belgian Promenade, a walkway built by grateful World War I refugees.

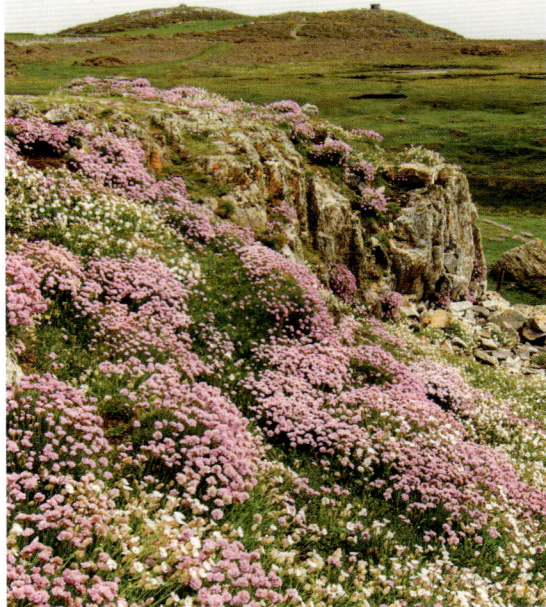

ABOVE: NEAR THE LOOKOUT STATION AT RHOSCOLYN. © ADAM LONG

BELOW: PORTH Y WYLFA, NEAR CEMAES, ANGLESEY. © TRACY BURTON

ABOVE: SOUTH STACK CLIFFS. © ADAM LONG
BELOW: RUNNING ACROSS SOUTH STACK CLIFFS NATURE RESERVE WITH HOLYHEAD MOUNTAIN IN THE BACKGROUND. © JEN & SIM BENSON

This stretch of the trail offers spectacular views of Snowdonia across the Menai Strait. A second bridge, the Britannia Bridge, was designed by Robert Stephenson. It was rebuilt after a group of teenagers, exploring inside it, accidentally set it alight in May 1970. At the foot of the bridge, the Coastal Path passes Llanfairpwllgwyngyllgogerychwyrndrobwllllantysiliogogogoch, a town with the longest place name in Europe. The town was the birthplace of Britain's Women's Institute and the first meeting of the organisation took place here in 1915.

A small detour from the route will take you to Bryn Celli Ddu, a passage tomb that visitors can enter. The path passes through the edge of Newborough Forest, past the tidal Llanddwyn Island. It was here that Dwynwen, unable to marry the man she loved, became a hermit and built a church in the fifth century. Much of the coastal path on Anglesey's western side hugs the golden sands of the coastline or traverses wide flat dunes, sometimes on boardwalks. The shining sands of Traeth Cymyran offer a route past the airfield at RAF Valley, where Prince William once served.

At Four Mile Bridge, the route passes back on to Holy Island. The Coastal Path saves one of its best sections for last, as it the cliffs rise higher and you follow a heathered path past dramatic sea stacks and arches. The white tower of South Stack Lighthouse tells you that you have almost returned to Holyhead, and you can climb to the top of the lighthouse if you wish. Another climb faces you, over Holyhead Mountain, Anglesey's largest hill – the Irish mountains of Wicklow can sometimes be seen from the summit. The route returns to Holyhead via North Stack and the Holyhead Breakwater Country Park.

The route may be walked at any time of year, although permissive paths may occasionally be closed and some of the cliff sections, particularly over Holyhead Mountain, may be slippery and exposed in winter. The Isle of Anglesey Coastal Path offers an opportunity to explore an entire island, rich in history and myth. It takes you past some of Wales' finest golden beaches and provides fantastic views of the Welsh coastline and the mountains of Snowdonia.

11 ISLE OF ANGLESEY COASTAL PATH: ESSENTIAL INFORMATION

TRAIL ESSENTIALS

Start:	**Holyhead, Anglesey, Wales**
End:	**Holyhead, Anglesey, Wales**
Distance:	**201km**
Ascent/descent:	**2,190m/2,190m**

HOW TO GET THERE

Holyhead has direct rail connections to London (Euston), Birmingham and Cardiff. Liverpool and Manchester are the closest international airports, although there is a direct rail link from Holyhead to Birmingham Airport. Holyhead also offers a ferry service to Dublin, Ireland.

TIME TO COMPLETE

Walking:	**8 days/50 hours**
Trekking:	**5 days/41 hours**
Fastpacking:	**4 days/31 hours**
Trail running:	**3 days/23 hours**

PROS

• **Sandy beaches** – the Coastal Path passes six Blue Flag Beaches on Anglesey, often offering you the opportunity to follow the path over them. Llanddwyn Island, Bull Bay and Church Bay are particular highlights.

• **Red squirrels** – grey squirrels have been eradicated from Anglesey, the last having been sighted in 2013, giving the red squirrel population a chance to thrive. The island is home to sixty per cent of all Welsh red squirrels, a population of approximately 700, and the Coastal Path through Newborough Forest is a good place to spot them.

• **Beaumaris** – this town offers a majestic royal castle, an historic gaol, a Victorian pier and plenty of good restaurants offering great local food.

CONS

• **Closures** – the route passes over permissive paths as well as public rights of way, and landowners may close these paths although diversions are usually signed – a section near Church Bay is closed between September and February each year, during the shooting season. Several sections of the path are only passable at low tide, and you may find yourself forced to take diversions along roads when the tide is too high.

• **Caravans** – Anglesey's beaches and wildlife attracts many summer tourists, and there are several caravan parks, positioned to enjoy the best seaside views, to pass en route.

GOOD TO KNOW

In May 1970, two teenagers were invited to a party but, when they got there, the party had been cancelled. Bored, they climbed into the Britannia Bridge, a rare example of a tubular bridge and the only rail connection to Anglesey. Improvising a torch by lighting discarded paper, they inadvertently set fire to the bridge. The tunnel within a tunnel construction of the bridge meant that it acted like a chimney and, despite the best efforts of fire crews on both sides of the Menai Strait, it could not be controlled. The subsequent reconstruction of the bridge, as a double-decked road and rail bridge, mean that the majestic limestone lions that guard each end of the bridge are no longer visible to most who travel over it now, although walkers on the Coastal Path can admire them.

FURTHER INFORMATION

www.visitanglesey.co.uk/en/about-anglesey/isle-of-anglesey-coastal-path

JAN	FEB	MAR	APR	MAY	JUN	JUL	AUG	SEP	OCT	NOV	DEC

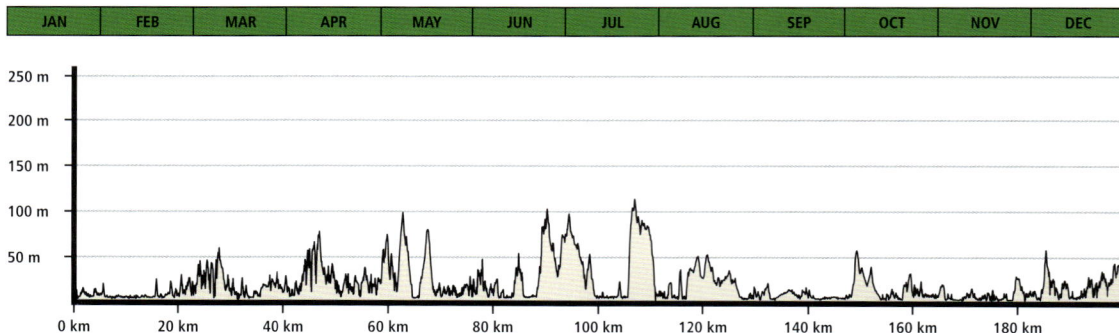

12 JOHN MUIR WAY – 213km

John Muir, John of the Mountains, was a naturalist and environmentalist. Born in Dunbar, his family moved to America when he was still a child. A passionate advocate of wilderness, he was responsible for the preservation of Yosemite and wrote movingly about his experiences in nature. In 2014, a 213-kilometre coast-to-coast route across his native Scotland linking his birthplace, Dunbar, with the point of his departure for the United States, Helensburgh, was created. This route is designed to be accessible, with no towering mountains or boggy mazes. It is a path that will let anyone who is able to walk a few kilometres at a time traverse a whole country and see some of the wild places of Scotland. Passing Loch Lomond, the Forth Bridge and through the heart of Edinburgh, this trail will show you some of Scotland's icons, and reveal the spirit of a country that drove Muir to love green spaces, blue skies and sea breezes.

Helensburgh, on Scotland's west coast, was a popular Victorian holiday resort and a welcome retreat from the dirty city for Glasgow's wealthier workers. It lies on the Highland Boundary Fault, the boundary between the Highlands and Lowlands, and was reputedly from where a young John Muir set sail for America with his family. The Way begins at a stone plinth on the seafront, near the pier.

The climb up Gouk Hill rewards you with spectacular views of the Trossachs and Loch Lomond. Balloch nestles at the foot of Loch Lomond, Britian's largest lake. The *Maid of the Loch*, built in 1953, was the last paddle steamer made in Scotland – it is moored at Balloch, and can be toured.

A conservation group have been working to enable it to sail again. The walk leaves Balloch via Balloch Castle Country Park; the castle built by a Glaswegian shipping magnate is now derelict, but the park is host to the annual Highland Games, as well as concerts and festivals.

At Carbeth, Allan Barns-Graham gave camping rights to soldiers returning from World War I, so that they could recuperate in the fresh air of the forest – this section of the route is largely on forestry tracks. From scrap and salvage, with socialist principles at the heart of the community, holiday huts were constructed on the site and, in 1941, they provided shelter to those fleeing bombing raids on Clydebank. The Carbeth Hutters – who, after bitter disputes with the landlord, bought the land in 2013 – were pioneers in minimalist, low-impact living.

From Strathblane, in the shadow of the Campsie Fells, the route follows a disused railway line, now part of the Sustrans National Cycle Network – the Way is also a cycle route, although walkers and cyclists sometimes have alternate routes. Kirkintilloch was once a fort on the Antonine Wall, a turf fortification which stretched from the Clyde to the Forth, and built as the northernmost border of the Roman Empire. Now Kirkintilloch is the 'Canal Capital of Scotland', and holds a canal festival every August – it is the Forth and Clyde Canal that will lead you out of the town. At Bar Hill, you'll discover more of the Antonine Wall as you climb to the Roman fort on the hilltop.

◀ LOOKING ACROSS LOCH LOMOND.
© WWW.WALKHIGHLANDS.CO.UK

THE FALKIRK WHEEL BOAT LIFT. © WWW.WALKHIGHLANDS.CO.UK

The route rejoins the canal near Auchinstarry Marina and leads you all the way to the Falkirk Wheel, the world's only rotating boat lift that was built in 2002 to reconnect the Forth and Clyde Canal with the higher Union Canal – a series of eleven locks had fallen into disrepair in the 1930s. You can enjoy a boat trip on it as it rotates over thirty metres into the air.

The fourteenth-century Callendar House, remodelled in the nineteenth century in the style of a French chateau, is now a museum, with information on the Antonine Wall and Falkirk's industrial past, as well as a cafe where you can enjoy an afternoon tea. You'll rejoin the Union Canal after leaving the estate – the house's owner, William Forbes, objected to the canal running through his estate, forcing the canal builders to tunnel through Prospect Hill. The Union Canal crosses the River Avon via a 250-metre-long aqueduct, the second longest in the United Kingdom – you'll leave the canal to follow a path along the river shortly after the aqueduct.

After Linlithgow, birthplace of Mary Queen of Scots, the route heads northwards towards the shores of the Firth of Forth, following an old fisherwomens' route through pleasant farmland. It reaches the Firth near Kinneil House. This sixteenth-century house was one home to Scotland's Regent, ruling in place of the infant Mary, and hosted James VI on several occasions. In the 1760s, Kinneil House was owned by John Roebuck, founder of the Carron Ironworks; it was in a cottage in the grounds, passed on the Way, that James Watt worked on his steam engine.

Blackness Castle, whose prow-like structure has earned it the nickname of 'the ship that never sailed', juts out over the Firth and was built as a fortress castle in the fifteenth century. When not obscured by the haar sea mist, you'll enjoy fine views of the bridges over the Firth of Forth. The stately home of Hopetoun House provides another picturesque location for afternoon tea. After passing under the iconic Forth Bridge at South Queensferry, the route diverts inland near Cramond – you'll soon reach the suburban streets of Edinburgh, passing the zoo, Murrayfield Stadium and the Water of Leith on the way. The tree-lined Meadows were once a loch, until it was drained in the seventeenth century.

The route through Holyrood Park, next to the Palace of Holyroodhouse and Scottish Parliament Building, does not climb over Arthur's Seat, but you might choose to summit this ancient volcano. The route rejoins the coast near Musselburgh, home to the world's oldest golf course. The nature reserves outside Prestonpans are ash mounds. This is a legacy of Cockenzie, one of Europe's dirtiest power stations, now demolished, leaving you to enjoy the golden beaches and sandy dunes.

North Berwick is famed for its seabirds – the nearby Bass Rock is home to the world's largest colony of northern gannets – so you might want to visit the Scottish Seabird Centre to find out more. As you cross the saltmarshes of Hedderwick Sands, the red cliffs of Dunbar will loom in front of you. The trail ends in the town of John Muir's birthplace, by the statue of him as a young boy outside John Muir's Birthplace museum.

The route begins close to Glasgow, and ends near to Edinburgh, both cities with international airports and good rail connections to the rest of the UK. You are usually close to a town with good travel connections, and you will find plenty of bed and breakfast and hotel accommodation en route. The route is never particularly high or exposed, and often follows canal towpaths, forestry tracks or shared cyclepaths. It can be walked at any time of year although, even in summer, you may be subjected to wind, rain and mist.

More than a hundred years ago, John Muir wrote 'Thousands of tired, nerve-shaken, over-civilised people are beginning to find out that going to the mountains is going home; that wilderness is a necessity'. The John Muir Way will allow you to discover the truth of those words, on the shoreline that first taught him to love nature.

ENJOYING VIEWS OF THE CAMPSIE FELLS. © WWW.WALKHIGHLANDS.CO.UK

12 JOHN MUIR WAY: ESSENTIAL INFORMATION

TRAIL ESSENTIALS

Start:	**Helensburgh, Dunbartonshire, Scotland**
End:	**Dunbar, East Lothian, Scotland**
Distance:	**213km**
Ascent/descent:	**1,830m/1,810m**
Also known as:	**Scotland's Coast to Coast**

HOW TO GET THERE

Helensburgh has train and bus services to Glasgow, which has an international airport. Helensburgh Central station is also on the Caledonian Sleeper route, an overnight rail service from Fort William to London.

Dunbar has a train station, on the East Coast Main Line, offering connections to Edinburgh and other Scottish cities.

TIME TO COMPLETE

Walking:	**9 days/51 hours**
Trekking:	**6 days/42 hours**
Fastpacking:	**4 days/32 hours**
Trail running:	**3 days/24 hours**

PROS

• **All year** – Scotland's snowy winters make much of its countryside less accessible during winter, and sometimes autumn. The John Muir Way is one of the few Scottish trails that can be attempted at any time of year.

• **Accessible** – this is a trail designed for anyone, with no steep climbs, no technical paths and few stiles. There is also a bridleway for those who would prefer to ride or cycle across Scotland.

• **Berwick coast** – the bird-rich, golden sands of North Berwick's sunny coast are one of Scotland's best-kept secrets.

CONS

• **The Central Belt** – this is not a route that climbs over Scotland's mountains or meanders through the glens. The Central Belt offers farmland, forests and canals.

• **Urban** – this is a route that passes through a large number of towns and villages, and you will sometimes find yourself skirting an industrial estate or walking through residential streets. There are lengthy road sections.

GOOD TO KNOW

John Muir is perhaps much more famous in the United States than in his native Scotland. A more challenging John Muir Trail traverses the Sierra Nevada mountain range in California. The 340-kilometre path passes through the Yosemite National Park and the Sequoia National Park, occasionally coinciding with the Pacific Crest Trail.

FURTHER INFORMATION

www.johnmuirway.org

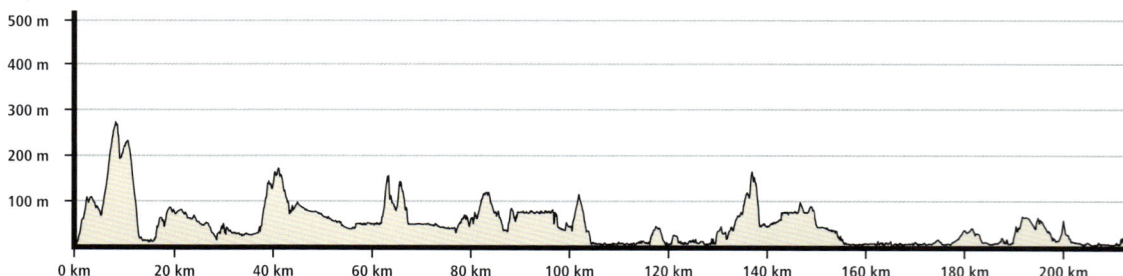

JAN	FEB	MAR	APR	MAY	JUN	JUL	AUG	SEP	OCT	NOV	DEC

Tyndrum
Crianlarich
Dundee
Perth
Crieff
Leuchars
St Andrews
Cupar
Auchterarder
Auchtermuchty
Callander
Crail
Loch Lomond and
The Trossachs National Park
Kinross
Glenrothes
Anstruther
Dunblane
M90
Buckhaven
Stirling
Alloa
Loch Lomond
Bannockburn
Kirkcaldy
Croftamie
M80
M9
Dunfermline
Kinghorn
Firth of Forth
North Berwick
Campsie Fells
Helensburgh
Balloch
Strathblane
Bonnybridge
Falkirk
Bo'ness
Dalgety Bay
Gullane
Polmont
Dunbar
Forth and Clyde Canal
Cockenzie and Port Seton
Dumbarton
Lennoxtown
M80
South Queensferry
M9
Edinburgh
Greenock
Cumbernauld
Linlithgow
Milngavie
Kirkintilloch
Musselburgh
Haddington
Erskine
M8
Livingston
Glasgow
Paisley
M8
Bonnyrigg
Penicuik
SCOTLAND
Pentland Hills
Hamilton
East Kilbride
M77
Strathaven
Moorfoot Hills
Kilwinning
Saltcoats
Lanark
N
Irvine
Kilmarnock
Peebles
M74
Biggar
Galashiels
Troon
Kelso
0
20 Kilometres
Ayr

13 KERRY WAY
– 202km

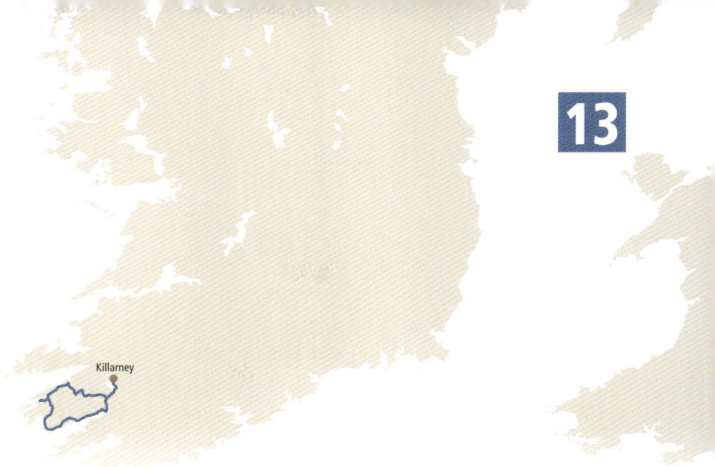

The 202-kilometre Kerry Way winds around the Iveragh Peninsula, over boggy mountain passes, along sandy beaches, past golf courses and crumbling cottages and stone circles. In the shadow of the Carrauntoohil, Ireland's highest mountain, along the historic butter roads; sometimes you'll enjoy the green hills that have nourished the Kerry cows, sometimes the sight of the wild Atlantic.

The Kerry Way starts in Killarney, very much a town that people pass through, on their way to the Ring of Kerry driving route or the Kerry Way National Trail, or the mountains and lakes and shores of the Iveragh Peninsula. Muckross Abbey, once under attack from marauders and Oliver Cromwell's forces, is now peaceful – the Franciscan friery's cloistered courtyard offers the shelter of a giant yew tree. The nearby Muckross House, built in 1843, hosted Queen Victoria in 1861 – the gift of the house and its grounds to the Irish State created the first national park in Ireland, and was the basis of the Killarney National Park.

As you walk the busy paths to the Torc Waterfall, you'll probably be overtaken by a horse-drawn jaunting carriage, whisking tourists around the local hotspots. A long Killarney tradition, generations of local *jarveys*, or carriage drivers, have passed the family firm from father to son for two centuries or more. The Torc Waterfall, its sparkling water dropping over mossy rocks amidst shady trees, is popular both with tourists and midges.

You'll join the busy former butter road Old Kenmare Road. The butter roads were built in the mid-eighteenth century, so that the farmers' salted butter could be quickly transported to Cork's Butter Exchange, where Kerry's dairy gold could be shipped as far as Australia and America. If you tire of the road, you can make a detour to climb Torc Mountain as you pass. Otherwise, you follow the Owengarriff River with the road, climbing to get your first glimpse of Carrauntoohil, at 1,039 metres Ireland's highest mountain and part of the MacGillycuddy's Reeks, which dominate the horizon for much of the Way.

You leave the road near the Crinnagh River to traverse boardwalks across marsh and, after a dense oak forest, the path splits – you must walk this spur again back to Killarney when you've closed the ring but, for now, your destination is the pretty stone Galway's Bridge, and then the Black Valley, passing Lord Brandon's Cottage, once a hunting lodge but now a restaurant.

As you walk around the base of Carrauntoohil, you'll be faced with ankle-twisting stony paths and treacherous marsh, and should the mountains be swirled in mist, you'll be grateful for a hot tea and slice of cake when you stumble across the isolated Cooky Monsters Cafe. This should fortify you for further climbs along Lack Road, another butter road, although more a path than track – you'll be rewarded with your first glimpses of the Dingle Peninsula, and the shining Lough Acoose beneath you.

◄ NEAR UPPER LAKE IN KILLARNEY NATIONAL PARK.
© JON BARTON

The Kerry Way does not give walkers a gentle start. It is on the Lack Road that you'll pass the highest point on the main route (385 metres), although the inland variation near Caherdaniel climbs higher. After Glencar, you'll face another steep climb to Windy Gap. The trail gets significantly easier after this, although there are still some climbs, particularly as you pass the Reeks again to return to Killarney.

Wynn's Castle, at Glenbeigh, was built by Baron Headley in 1867 – as costs spiralled and rents rose, more and more of his tenants were evicted. The coast here offers great views across to the Dingle Peninsula on mist-free days. A disused railway line leads you to the climb over Drung Hill, the first of several climbs on this section – you can see the Ring of Kerry road winding around the coast below you.

Near Foilmore, home to one of Ireland's most successful Gaelic football teams, there is a spur down to Cahersiveen. The church here is the only one in Ireland named after a layperson, Daniel O'Connell, the Liberator, who campaigned for Catholic emancipation and an independent Ireland.

After a tough, boggy ridge walk, you have two alternatives routes to O'Connell's hometown of Caherdaniel. The mountain route will take you high over another Windy Gap, even higher than the first (392 metres), as it skirts Eagles Hill. The coastal route is a pleasant brackened path through the seaside town of Waterville. Now a popular angling and golfing destination, Waterville was Charlie Chaplin's preferred family holiday destination in the 1960s. Its position on Ireland's south-western tip meant it was chosen as the terminus for the first ever telegraph link between Europe and North America.

IN THE SHADOW OF THE CAHER MOUNTAIN. © JON BARTON

VIEW FROM THE MACGILLYCUDDY'S REEKS. © JON BARTON

Caherdaniel once stood on the butter road, but now it is home to the Sun, the start of the Way of the Planets – along three and a half kilometres of the Way, steel balls representing each planet in the Solar System have been positioned. This sculpture celebrates the Kerry International Dark Sky Reserve, Ireland's first Dark Sky Reserve and one of only four gold-tier reserves in the world. Just off the green, wooded path between Caherdaniel and Sneem stands Staigue Fort. No one knows who built this stone ring fort, or cashel, the largest in Ireland, but it is generally dated to between 100BC and AD400.

Sneem is famous for its square black (blood) pudding, which is baked rather than boiled, and now has EU Protected Designation Origin. Charles de Gaulle chose Sneem as his holiday destination in 1969 when he needed a quiet place to recuperate after resigning the French presidency. A flatter coastal route follows shaded forest paths towards Blackwater Bridge. The Reeks are your constant companion on this section, and the route takes a hilly diversion into Kenmare, where you might encounter Beara Way walkers.

The route enters the town close to the Kenmare Stone Circle; this fifteen-stoned Bronze Age circle is one of Ireland's largest. There is also a fairy tree here, where you might make a wish for good weather, or dry boots at least. Some choose to finish the Way in this pleasant market town, with its pub-lined streets. Those who continue face a steep climb over the third Windy Gap en route, through the Killarney National Park. You'll find yourself back near Galway's Bridge, from where you retrace the spur into Killarney.

The Kerry Way was Ireland's second National Trail, and remains one of its most popular, so walkers and runners will find a tourist infrastructure designed to meet their needs. There is plenty of bed and breakfast accommodation and small hotels en route although budget travellers will also find a reasonable number of campsites and hostels.

Although the Way might be attempted in winter, you may find some of the longer sections a challenge for short days, particularly in bad weather. Many bed and breakfasts close over winter, and bus services stop or offer very reduced services.

At times, you may curse the boggy paths on the Kerry Way that seem to drag you backwards. The mist from the sea will mingle with the mist that rises from the mountains, to chill your bones. But there is always an unexpected joy waiting for just over the next mountain pass, be that a beautiful green valley, a pretty seaside town or an unpredictably sunny day. The serpentine humps of this challenging route, which traverses the wildest scenery of Ireland's coast and mountains, will leave you breathless, sometimes with delight.

13 KERRY WAY: ESSENTIAL INFORMATION

TRAIL ESSENTIALS

Start: **Killarney, County Kerry, Ireland**
End: **Killarney, County Kerry, Ireland**
Distance: **202km**
Ascent/descent: **4,700m/4,700m**

HOW TO GET THERE

Killarney has rail connections to Dublin and Cork, which offer international air and ferry connections. Although Kerry Airport is closer, it offers only limited flight services to the United Kingdom and Europe.

TIME TO COMPLETE

Walking: **10 days/62 hours**
Trekking: **6 days/50 hours**
Fastpacking: **5 days/38 hours**
Trail running: **4 days/27 hours**

PROS

- **Bed and breakfasts** – you can expect a friendly welcome from the reasonably priced bed and breakfasts along the Kerry Way. Your overnight stay will include a hearty breakfast, of local produce, and in remoter areas you may be able to purchase an evening meal too.

- **Mountain views** – while the Kerry Way does not summit the mountains, you are often in the shadow of spectacular mountain scenery, particularly the MacGillycuddy's Reeks.

CONS

- **Terrain** – the Kerry Way gives you plenty of opportunity to experience Ireland's peaty bogs. But the butter roads may not offer much relief; these are often ankle-jarring stony paths rather than well-laid tracks.

- **Tourist trail** – Kerry is Ireland's most popular tourist destination, and you may well be run-over by a jaunting carriage before you leave Killarney in the summer. As well as hikers on the trail, towns around the peninsula may be busy with tourist driving the Ring of Kerry road.

- **Seaside** – the Kerry Way does not hug the coast as much as you might expect. While you do get the opportunity to relax in pleasant seaside towns at the end of the day, the route often prefers to hug the mountainsides rather than follow beaches or cliffs.

GOOD TO KNOW

The Skellig Islands lie west of the Ivergh Peninsula, and can be visited by boat from Waterville or Caherdaniel. These bird-rich rocky outcrops were once the site of an early Christian monastery, but more recently have been the backdrop for *The Force Awakens* and *The Last Jedi* Star Wars films. If you visit between April and August, you may glimpse Kerry's famous puffins.

FURTHER INFORMATION

www.sportireland.ie/outdoors/walking/trails/kerry-way

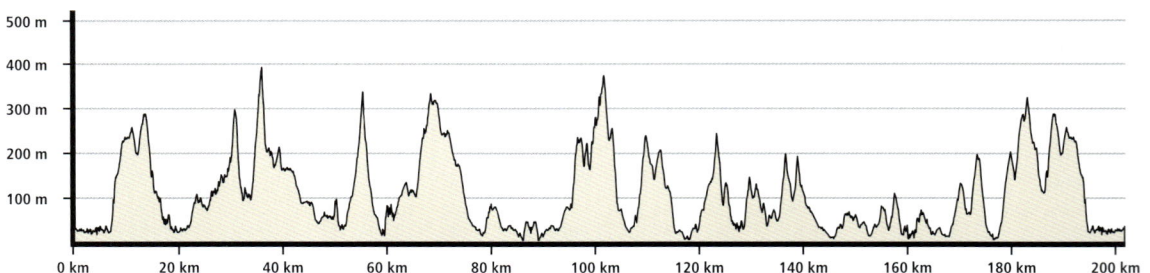

JAN	FEB	MAR	APR	MAY	JUN	JUL	AUG	SEP	OCT	NOV	DEC

Killarney **S F**

Muckross Lake

Torc Mountain ▲

Mangerton ▲

R569

Kenmare

Kenmare Stone Circle ◇

Glengarriff

Lough Leane

N72

Upper Lake

Purple Mountain ▲

IRELAND

Templenoe

Beara peninsula

Coomadiha ▲

Adrigole

Mangerton ▲

Strickeen ▲

Beenkeragh ▲

Carrauntoohil ▲

Choc na Toinne ▲

Maolán Buí ▲

Broaghnabinnia ▲

Stumpa Dúloigh ▲

R568

Knockmoyle ▲

Knocknagullion ▲

Kenmare Bay

Tuosist

Lauragh

Hungry Hill ▲

R571

Macgillycuddy's Reeks

Lough Acoose

Glencar

Lough Caragh ▼

Beenn ▲

Iveragh peninsula

Coomura Mtn ▲

An Corrán ▲

Knocknagantee ▲

Sneem

Ardgroom

Eyeries

N70

Seefin ▲

Glenbeigh

Meentog ▲

Coomacarrea ▲

Derriana Lough

Coomcallee ▲

An Bheann Mhór ▲

Iskraghanny Lough

Castlecove

Beenn Hill ▲

Kells Mtn ▲

Knocknadobar ▲

Derrynane ▲

Foilclogh ▼

Lough Currane

Eagles Hill ▲

Farraniaragh Mountain ▲

Caherdaniel

Dingle Bay

Cahersiveen

Waterville

Knightstown

Baile an Sceilg

Chapeltown

Portmagee

N ←○

10 Kilometres

0

14 LONDON LOOP
– 230km

Even the city dweller can find outdoor adventure on their doorstep; every city has its secret green spaces, and the traces of those who lived before hidden in its parks and buildings. The 230-kilometre London LOOP (London Outer Orbital Path) has its fair share of suburban streets, dual carriageways and golf courses. It is sometimes blighted by litter, sewage works and rubbish dumps. But there are enough bluebell woodlands, grassy hills and golden farmers' fields to make anyone fall in love with London again. You'll follow London's smaller rivers, encounter the city's wildlife and discover hidden histories. These fields and forests on the city's very edge were once the playground of kings and queens, but now are yours to enjoy.

The London LOOP is not quite a circle – an uncrossable stretch of the Thames separates Erith from Purfleet. The start of the route – past scrapyards and recycling centres, on to desolate marshland – might be enough to deter the less determined walker. It's worth a short detour off route to enjoy the gardens of Hall Place, a Tudor manor with a chequered history – at various times, home of the bacchanalian Hellfire Club's founder, Francis Dashwood, a boarding school and a code breakers intercept station. Now it houses a museum, but the pleasant gardens include the unusual topiary Queen's Beasts, trimmed in the shape of the sculptures that marked the Queen's coronation.

After a scenic stroll under weeping willows along the River Cray, you'll reach the Scadbury Park Nature Reserve. In the middle of the park, you'll pass the moated manor, rebuilt in Tudor times. Petts Wood, an ancient woodland of ash, oak and birch, was once the source of timber for nearby shipyards but, in the face of London's expansion, was saved for the nation by the National Trust in 1927. It was concern about London's rapid expansion in the 1920s that provoked the discussions that led to the concept of the green belt, a policy developed by Herbert Morrison for the London County Council in the 1930s. It's this green girdle which still encircles London today that enables the London LOOP to exist.

Near Keston, you'll pass the remains of the Wilberforce Oak where Pitt the Younger and William Wilberforce discussed the abolition of slavery; a bench now marks the site. More historic oaks await you on West Wickham Common – the Domesday Oaks are believed to be at least 700 years old.

The London LOOP is largely flat, but the climb up to the Addington Hills viewpoint rewards you with views of the distant Thames, the towers of Canary Wharf, the Millennium Dome – on a clear day, you might even be able to make out Windsor Castle. The grassy chalkland undulations of Happy Valley and cattle-strewn heathland of Farthing Downs could make you forget you're only a few kilometres south of Croydon.

◀ A WALK IN THE WOODS NEAR BOGEY LANE.
© GAURAV CHANDRA

ENFIELD LOCK NO.13 AND COTTAGES ON THE RIVER LEE NAVIGATION. © ANDREW LEWIS

Near Coulsdon, you may notice the uniform semi-detached houses of Little Woodcote – these were 'homes for heroes', built for the returning soldiers of World War I, each at the centre of their own smallholdings. In summer, you'll smell Mayfield Lavender Farm long before you see it. Once a Victorian lavender field, in 2004 acres and acres of organic lavender were planted here, originally for Yardley perfume. You could pop into the giftshop and treat yourself to some lavender-flavoured chocolate.

You'll walk through Nonsuch Park where Henry VIII, never a monarch to lack ambition, built the palace to beat all others, Nonsuch Palace. It stood for only 144 years. Charles II gifted it to his mistress, Barbara Villiers, who pulled it down to pay off her gambling debts. The path follows the Hogsmill River from its source in Ewell down to Kingston upon Thames – it was this river, near Malden Manor, that provided the backdrop for John Everett Millais's painting *Ophelia*.

Kingston upon Thames – or king's town – has always been associated with royalty and, as you reach the borough, you'll cross the twelfth-century Clattern Bridge, named for the clattering of horses' hooves over it, to reach the Anglo-Saxon

Coronation Stone. The Coronation Stone, site of the coronation of seven Anglo-Saxon kings, was for many years used as a horse-mounting block in the market square.

You'll cross the Thames at Kingston, to pass through Henry VIII's royal hunting ground of Bushy Park, now famous for its deer. The more urban Crane Park was once the location of Hounslow Gunpowder Mills. This dangerous industry, the cause of many dramatic explosions, was located here from the sixteenth century. Only the Shot Tower remains, and on Sundays visitors can climb to the top.

The riverside paths by the River Crane through Hounslow and Hatton Cross offer a surprise urban respite from Heathrow. Near Cranford Park, the route leaves the river to join the Grand Union Canal – the canal will take you past Uxbridge's business parks and golf courses. Near Harrow, Grim's Dyke, named for the prehistoric earthwork, is a hotel and golf course now, but was once the home of W.S. Gilbert, composer Sullivan's theatrical partner.

Bentley Priory was an RAF headquarters; the Battle of Britain was coordinated from here. The woods here, now dissected by busy dual carriageways, are the remnants of the once giant Forest of Middlesex. Near Barnet, the route passes across Enfield Chase, another royal hunting ground. It crosses the New River, which is not a river but a canal, built in 1613, to carry clean drinking water into the centre of London.

Another water crossing takes place at Enfield Lock, next to which once stood the Royal Gunpowder Mills and the Royal Small Arms Factory (where the eponymous rifles were made). The route now enters Lee Valley Park – first conceived of in the 1940s, this park was a triumph of the regeneration of post-war London, a reclamation of derelict land. More recently, parts were used to create the 2012 Olympic Park. The sporting history continues as you pass the Scout Association's headquarters at Gilwell Park, and enter Epping Forest by Elizabeth I's hunting lodge – the LOOP offers muddy paths through the medieval forest. This marks a return to a more rural section of the LOOP, through Essex's farmland and, in Havering Park, an avenue of giant redwoods.

You'll pass close to the white sails of Upminster Windmill before making a bleak return to the Thames near the Tilda rice factory. Sinking into the river here are the concrete barges – these were built to carry fuel during the Normandy landings, when steel was in short supply. By the barges, a lonely figure stares out across the Thames, back towards Erith when your journey began. This is the modern sculpture, The Diver; it is completely submerged during the highest tides. Past Coldharbour Point, the LOOP takes a more pleasant path through Rainham Marshes. Once the property of the Ministry of Defence, they are now an RSPB nature reserve, and you may spot peregrine falcons, lapwings or water voles en route to the LOOP's end at Purfleet.

Most who walk the LOOP choose not to walk it all at once, but rather to spend a sunny afternoon in the shade of ancient forests or, on a crisp winter's day, to let the way-markers guide them down frosted riverbanks. It is the perfect trail for the tourist who wants a few days' respite from London's busy streets, an opportunity to discover the suburbs that Londoners live in.

14 LONDON LOOP: ESSENTIAL INFORMATION

TRAIL ESSENTIALS

Start:	**Erith, Greater London, England**
End:	**Purfleet, Essex, England**
Distance:	**230km**
Ascent/descent:	**1,840m/1,840m**
Also known as:	**London Outer Orbital Path**

HOW TO GET THERE

Erith is on the Southeastern rail network; there are direct trains from London's central Charing Cross and Cannon Street stations. London's airports are the closest international airports, and Eurostar (from London St Pancras) offers direct continental train services.

Purfleet is on the London to Southend-on-Sea railway, and there are direct trains to London's central Fenchurch Street Station.

TIME TO COMPLETE

Walking:	**9 days/55 hours**
Trekking:	**6 days/45 hours**
Fastpacking:	**5 days/34 hours**
Trail running:	**4 days/26 hours**

PROS

- **History** – the route passes historic homes, royal parks and key industrial revolution sites. You'll discover ancient earthworks, London's disappeared Tudor palace and World War II turrets and pillboxes.

- **Public transport** – the LOOP is one of Transport for London's seven strategic walking routes. They publish guides to each of the twenty-four sections of the route that detail the public transport links to each section. This makes it the perfect route to do on day trips from central London.

- **Rivers** – from Millais's Hogsmill, along the meadows of the pretty Cray, by the muddy banks of the Crane as it threads through Hounslow's busy streets, this route will take you over and along the rivers that flow into the Thames, the waters that quenched London's thirsty workers, and that gave the suburbs their names.

CONS

- **Suburbia** – while the route takes every opportunity to visit the forests, parks and hidden green spaces of the city, it has more than its fair share of suburban streets, local high streets and tarmac pounding.

- **Industry** – past the business estate of Stockley Park, the Thameside Tilda rice factory, the car breakers of Erith, there are plenty of opportunities to admire London's most functional industrial architecture.

- **Golf courses** – some Big Trails meander from pub to pub; the LOOP sometimes feels like a circuit around London's golf courses. It travels alongside, often crossing, more than a dozen golf courses.

GOOD TO KNOW

In May 2019, *Runner's World* assembled a crack team of runners, including Olympian Andy Baddley, barefoot running athlete Anna McNuff and Kate Carter, the fastest woman to run a marathon in a panda costume. Their aim – to run a London LOOP relay in twenty-four hours. Unluckily, they narrowly failed, completing the LOOP in twenty-four hours and twenty-two minutes, although had it not been for some accidental night-time detours, they might have run the LOOP in a day.

FURTHER INFORMATION

www.tfl.gov.uk/modes/walking/loop-walk;
The London Loop (Aurum Press, 2017).

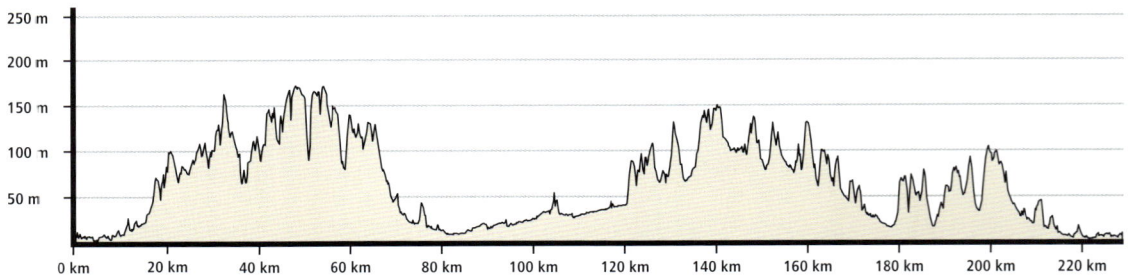

JAN	FEB	MAR	APR	MAY	JUN	JUL	AUG	SEP	OCT	NOV	DEC

Luton

LUTON

Harpenden

Welwyn Garden City

Ware

BISHOP'S STORTFORD

STANSTED

A1(M)

Hemel Hempstead

St Albans

ENGLAND

Hoddesdon
Broxbourne

Harlow

M11

Chipping Ongar

M1

M25

Potters Bar

Waltham Cross

Epping

Watford

Elstree

Chipping Barnet

Cockfosters

Enfield

Loughton

Brentwood

Rickmansworth

Northwood

Edgware

Buckhurst Hill

Chigwell

Harefield

East Finchley

Walthamstow

Romford

s Cross

Ruislip

Harrow

Upminster

M25

Wembley

Eurostar

Rainham

M25

Uxbridge

Southall

London

River Thames

Purfleet

Grays

M4

Grand Union Canal

Hammersmith

Woolwich

Erith

Hayes

Hounslow

Brixton

Sidcup

Bexley

Dartford

HEATHROW

Hatton

Teddington

Bromley

Petts Wood

Swanley

Staines-upon-Thames

River Thames

Kingston upon Thames

Croydon

West Wickham

Orpington

M25

M20

Ewell

Sutton

Addington Hills

Biggin Hill

N o r t h   D o w n s

oking

Cobham

Epsom

Banstead

Farthing Downs

Coulsdon

Warlingham

Sevenoaks

Leatherhead

M25

M25

Oxted

ord

N

Dorking

Redhill

M23

Horley

0   10 Kilometres

Gatwick

LIVERPOOL
Chester
Hereford
Newport
BRISTOL

15 OFFA'S DYKE
PATH – 287km

The 287-kilometre Offa's Dyke Path meanders along the border of England and Wales, following Offa's Dyke, the longest ancient earthwork in Britain. The trail often leaves the historic monument to take advantage of the view from a hill, visit historic border towns or wander along rivers. This sometimes level, sometimes hilly, sometimes heathered, sometimes forested trail is never boring. Marches are border country; they are the land between countries, and the Welsh Marches, through which the trail traverses, are defined by being where Wales met Mercia. There are castles and forts to be discovered, but also places of play, where two countries came together. This route is not the wildest, but it is also not as easy as it may seem, and it proves that it is in the edgelands that the best adventures are to be had.

Offa's Dyke Path begins in the Forest of Dean, at Sedbury Cliffs where the River Wye meets the River Severn. With the Severn Bridge behind you, you'll enjoy a good view of the earthworks as you head towards the castle town of Chepstow. On the outskirts of the town, you'll pass Pen Moel, an impressive early Arts and Crafts house. The route here follows the River Wye, and you'll enjoy a great view of the river from Wintour's Leap. According to local legend, the Royalist Sir John Wintour, who was being pursued on horseback by Parliamentary forces, leapt from his horse into the river to swim to safety at Chepstow Castle.

Another clifftop viewing point is Devil's Pulpit, that lets you look down towards the ruins of Tintern Abbey. Near Brockweir, at the tidal reach of the Wye, you can choose to drop down to the river or stay on the wooded hilltops. Both paths reunite to follow a path high above the river into Monmouth. Monmouth was at the centre of the turmoil between Henry III and his barons, and you can still walk across the Monnow Bridge, the only fortified bridge with a gate tower in Britain, and one of only three in Europe. A pleasant wooded path offers views of the distant Brecon Beacons. Oaks give way to apple trees – the large orchard grows fruit for Bulmers cider.

White Castle, near Llantilio Crossenny, was one of the three castles that protected the route from Wales to Hereford. Rudolf Hess, who was imprisoned in Abergavenny, used to visit the ruins to sketch. You'll enjoy fine views of the sharp peak of the Skirrid as you walk down towards Pandy. The Path climbs to its highest point, on the Hatterrall Ridge of the Black Mountains, where it briefly meets the Beacons Way – this is one of several occasions when the path chooses to divert from the Dyke in order to enjoy the surrounding countryside, here offering a fine heathery ridge walk with views over the Black Mountains and Brecon Beacons.

The route descends again into Hay-on-Wye, home to the famous literary festival and more than twenty bookshops. A gentle climb allows you to enjoy views of the Brecon Beacons and the more distant Malvern Hills. After crossing the high Hergest Ridge, inspiration for musician Mike Oldfield, you'll descend into Kington. Here, Hergest Court

◀ TRAIL RUNNING ON THE FLANKS OF HAY BLUFF IN THE BLACK MOUNTAINS.
© JOHN COEFIELD

is reputedly haunted by the huge bloodhound Black Vaughan; this spectral beast is believed to have provided inspiration to Arthur Conan Doyle when he visited before writing *The Hound of the Baskervilles*.

Leaving Kington, the trail follows the Dyke through some of the most beautiful of the Welsh Marches. You should be on your guard for flying golf balls as you cross Bradnor Hill – the golf course is the highest in England. You follow a wooded path past the Iron Age Burfa Hillfort before passing through cornfields and pastures to reach Knighton, home of the Offa's Dyke Association. If you want to discover more about the history of the Dyke, the Association's Offa's Dyke Centre in Knighton, nearly at the halfway point of the trail, is free to visit (and has a cake-rich cafe).

The switchback section between Knighton and Montgomery as the route crosses the Shropshire Hills involves unrelenting ascents and descents, and many believe it to be the toughest part of the Path. At the hillfort at Beacon Ring, a tribute to the Queen's coronation is hidden in the trees. You have conquered the hills and now a flatter section, following the River Severn through Welshpool and along a canal, offers some respite for weary legs.

The Path soon climbs again towards Oswestry Racecourse – eccentric MP John 'Mad Jack' Mytton raced his horses at this once popular course, which closed in 1848. The majestic Chirk Castle was continuously inhabited for nearly 700 years, but is now looked after by the National Trust – the toparied, rose-rich gardens are worth a detour. This countryside still bears the scars of mining and quarrying, although butterflies adore the now grassy quarries.

LOOKING DOWN ON THE RIVER WYE NEAR SYMOND'S YAT. © ADAM LONG

You can choose to follow the River Dee or detour across the Pontcysyllte Aqueduct, the largest aqueduct in Britain. It was designed by Thomas Telford to carry the canal across the river, and is now a World Heritage Site. Every five years, the plug is pulled and the water drains from the aqueduct into the Dee below to allow for inspection and maintenance. It is this section by Llangollen where you leave the earthwork Offa's Dyke behind you for good.

Near Llangollen, under the ruins of Castell Dinas Brân, the path passes through the narrow valley of World's End. You are not yet at trail's end though, as the Offa's Dyke Path still has some hills for you to climb as it passes over the heathered Clwydian Range. On a fine day you may be able to see the distant mountains of Snowdonia. The route takes you past several iron hillforts and the remains of the Jubilee Tower on Moel Famau, the highest peak in the Clwydian Range. The tower was built to celebrate the golden jubilee of George III in 1810.

The hills become smaller as the route prepares to descend into Prestatyn. With the sea now on the horizon, you pass through the Valley of the Mills, which once hummed with cloth and flour mills. As you reach the outskirts of Prestatyn, a bronzed sculpture of a giant Roman helmet sinks into the hillside. Another sculpture, a stainless steel sun, the Dechrau A Diwedd ('beginning and end', although the locals have nicknamed it the Polo mint), marks the trail's end on Prestatyn's golden beach. It is traditional for finishers to wash their weary feet in the sea.

The route may be walked at any time of year, although the highest hills might be challenging in winter. While the trail passes many pleasant towns and villages, there are some stretches with limited shops and villages, and some face a few long days on the trail. The Path links the two ends of the Wales Coast Path, offering the unique opportunity to walk around an entire country. Many choose to walk the Offa's Dyke Path in sections, and there is good reason to – this is one of the most varied National Trails, and everyone will find a section to delight them.

15 OFFA'S DYKE PATH: ESSENTIAL INFORMATION

TRAIL ESSENTIALS

Start:	**Sedbury Cliffs, near Chepstow, Gloucester-shire on the English–Welsh border**
End:	**Prestatyn, Denbighshire, Wales**
Distance:	**287km**
Ascent/descent:	**7,650m/7,660m**

HOW TO GET THERE

Chepstow has direct rail connections to Birmingham and Cardiff – Cardiff is the closest international airport. Connections to other rail services, including towards London, can be made at Cheltenham Spa.

Prestatyn offers direct rail connections to Birmingham and Manchester – the closest international airports are at Manchester and Liverpool. You will usually have to make one or more changes to reach Cardiff or London.

TIME TO COMPLETE

Walking:	**15 days/92 hours**
Trekking:	**9 days/75 hours**
Fastpacking:	**7 days/56 hours**
Trail running:	**5 days/40 hours**

PROS

• **Varied** – the route passes from shore to shore, taking you along rivers, over hills, through ancient forests and historical industry. The trail swiftly changes from steep climbs to flat canals, and back again.

• **Castles** – in addition to many ancient hillforts, you also pass White, Llangollen, Chirk and Chepstow Castles. Should you yearn for more castles, you can even sleep in one – the St Briavels Youth Hostel is in a (haunted) Norman castle.

CONS

• **Accommodation** – there may be twenty kilometres or more between accommodation options, particularly in the more northerly sections of the trail. You would be well advised to be flexible – there is some bed and breakfast accommodation along most of the route, but budget travellers may have to switch between hostels and campsites.

• **Stiles** – Offa's Dyke Path was notorious for its many stiles, including the distinctive stone stiles near Prestatyn. Many have now been replaced, but often with optimistically narrow kissing gates.

GOOD TO KNOW

Unusually, the record for completing Offa's Dyke Path is jointly held by a woman and a man, Nia Albiston and Gordon Hughes, who were the only finishers in a team of four in March 2019. The trail runners from North Wales ran to raise money for the Wales Air Ambulance service and finished in sixty-three hours and one minute.

FURTHER INFORMATION

www.offasdyke.org.uk

JAN	FEB	MAR	APR	MAY	JUN	JUL	AUG	SEP	OCT	NOV	DEC

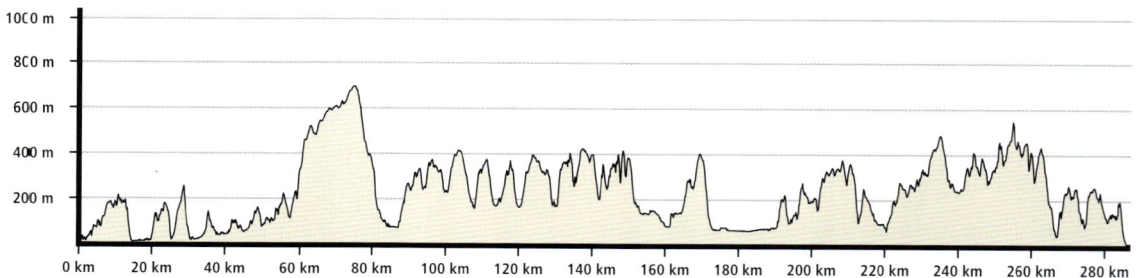

NORWICH

16 PEDDARS WAY AND NORFOLK COAST PATH
– 214km

The 214-kilometre Peddars Way and Norfolk Coast Path is the National Trail where you get two paths for the price of one. The Peddars Way takes the arrow-straight path of a Roman, or older, track from the heart of Norfolk to the sea, through gentle farmland. This quiet part of England is one of the longest-inhabited areas in England; from Bronze Age tumuli to Norman fortifications and medieval priories, you'll see the history of this inhabitation around you. After the solitude of songbird-strewn trails, the bustle of Norfolk's seaside resorts may be a shock. But you'll still find plenty of quiet coastline as you walk the sandy beaches and grassy dunes of north Norfolk's beautiful coast path.

The Peddars Way begins at Knettishall Heath, about five kilometres outside Thetford. It follows the route of a Roman road, built after the defeat of Boudicca, Queen of the Iceni, although some say that the road is even older than that. It will lead you from the Norfolk–Suffolk border to Norfolk's northern coast although, as with many National Trails, it starts inauspiciously enough in a car park. The Way skirts Thetford Forest, the largest lowland pine forest in Britain and a popular mountain biking destination – the forest is a modern creation, planted in the 1920s and 1930s, as part of a job creation scheme in this hard-hit rural area.

The trail leads through the Brecks, an area of sandy heathland, traditionally planted for a few years and then allowed to return to heath. Although many areas are now forested, the apparently barren heathland harbours a diverse range of flora and fauna, including the rare native

golden pheasant. While the trail passes through several small villages and hamlets, few have any shops although many still have traditional pubs.

Near Thompson Water, you will pass the Norfolk Songline sculpture, one of several en route that celebrate the Peddars Way. The route here passes pingos and small freshwater lakes, some of which are natural and some created by farmers. The route also follows roads and tracks through Norfolk farmland. In Little Cressingham, you'll pass a rare wind and watermill, and in Castle Acre, you'll pass under the Norman bailey gate. The ruins of the Cluniac priory at Castle Acre, a victim of Henry VIII, are a reminder of Norfolk's rich religious heritage.

The Peddars Way takes a straight route to the coast with little to distract you other than the Bronze Age tumuli at Harpley Common and the ancient burial grounds at Amner Minque. The route skirts the royal Sandringham Estate. Near Sedgeford, you'll pass a holiday cottage – it looks like an old chapel, but it is a magazine built in disguise to store Cromwell's ammunition. After Ringstead, where you say goodbye to the Roman road, you get your first glimpse of the sandy Norfolk coast.

The Peddars Way finishes at Holme next the Sea, but to complete the Norfolk Coast Path you must walk south-west along the coast to Hunstanton, and then retrace your steps back to Holme next the Sea, although you can at least walk along the beach at low tide. Hunstanton,

◀ APPROACHING SHERINGHAM ON THE NORFOLK COAST PATH.
© ANNA PAXTON

THE NORTH SEA, NORFOLK COAST. © ANNA PAXTON

w th its striped cliffs, is the only resort in the eastern England to face west, making it one of the few places on the east coast where you can watch the sun set over the sea. You may spot egrets, redshanks or pied avocets on the grassy path through the Holme Dunes nature reserve.

Brancaster is a great place to stop for lunch if you enjoy lobster or crab, as Brancaster Staithe is still a busy fishing po t. You can also visit the Roman fort of Branodunum, just outside the village. As you cross the goose-dense Deepdale Marshes, you'll see the windmill at Burnham Overy towering in front of you – it's now bunkhouse holiday accommodation, owned by the National Trust, although it has a three-night minimum stay. The path towards Wells-next-the-Sea is along the golden beach.

The path to Blakeney Point is through endless saltmarshes – there is a colony of approximately 500 seals near this sand spit. Between Cley next the Sea, with another windmill, and Sheringham, sand gives way to shingle beaches, dotted with World War II defences. At Sheringham, you could pause for a steam train ride along the North Norfolk Railway.

The path rises over cliffs now, to climb to Beeston Bump, the highest point in Norfolk (at sixty-three metres). It was on these cliffs that the West Runton Elephant, the largest near-complete mammoth skeleton, was found on a stormy night in 1990. The route winds down through caravan parks to the popular resort of Cromer, famous for its delicious brown crabs.

You might follow the beach to Mundesley, but only at the lowest of tides. Otherwise it is a grassy clifftop walk, past small coppices and the golf ball radar station at RAF Trimingham. There are more caravan parks to negotiate as you head towards the red-striped Happisburgh Lighthouse, once one of a pair, built in the eighteenth century after seventy ships were lost at sea during a winter storm. Past California (in Hemsby), the path progresses to the lifeboat station at Caister-on-Sea – a monument commemorates the nine crewmen who were lost here in the 1901 lifeboat disaster, giving rise to the saying 'Caister men never turn back'.

The route promenades through the popular seaside town of Great Yarmouth, although those expecting 'the finest place in the universe' (as it is described in Dickens'

CLIFFTOP VIEWS BETWEEN SHERINGHAM AND CROMER ON THE NORFOLK COAST.
© ANNA PAXTON

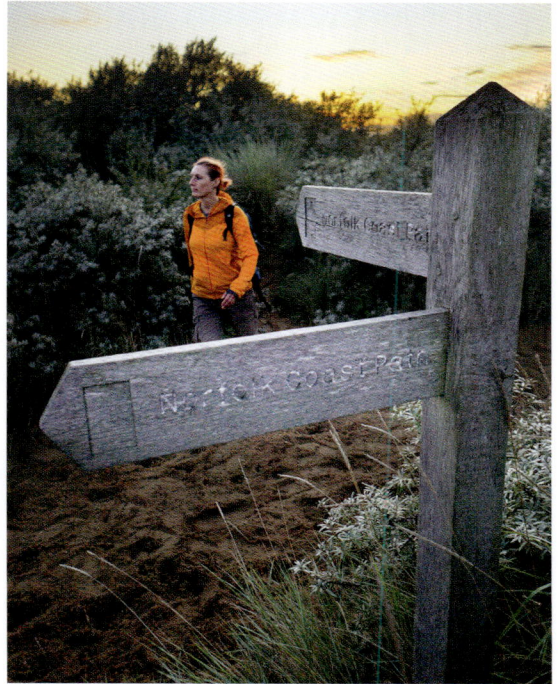
HOLME DUNES, SOUTH OF HUNSTANTON ON THE NORFOLK COAST PATH.
© ANNA PAXTON

David Copperfield) may be disappointed. This ancient town was the target of Britain's first air raid, by a Zeppelin in 1915, and was subsequently frequently bombed as the last place passed over by German planes returning home in World War II. Despite this destruction, Great Yarmouth's Golden Mile, twin piers and newly restored Venetian Waterways still lure thousands of happy tourists every year. Depending on the tide, you may take a grassy cliff path or stroll along the sandy beaches to reach Gorleston-on-Sea, and then journey's end at Hopton on Sea.

The Peddars Way and Norfolk Coast Path may be walked at any time of year, and Norfolk has some of the most clement weather in England. Although it has neither the hottest summers nor coldest winters, it has been subject to winter storms and flooding and in bad weather – the flat terrain can leave you exposed. The rapid coastal erosion may cause the path to be diverted. While there are plenty of campsites and bed and breakfasts en route, hostel accommodation is limited, particularly on the Peddars Way section, and accommodation options may be more limited in the winter. The Peddars Way is the last link in the Greater Ridgeway, an ancient route stretching from Dorset to Norfolk.

The royals appreciate the gentle charms of North Norfolk – the queen retreats to her private estate at Sandringham each winter, and Kate and William have a home just down the road in Amner. But this wide, flat farmland and sandy coast under impossibly vast blue skies is perhaps one of England's undiscovered treasures.

TRAIL ESSENTIALS

Start:	**Knettishall Heath, Suffolk, England**
End:	**Hopton on Sea, Norfolk, England**
Distance:	**214km**
Ascent/descent:	**1,040m/1,060m**

HOW TO GET THERE

Knettishall Heath is served by buses from Thetford, where rail connections to London, generally via Cambridge, can be made. In addition to London's airports, international connections can be made to Rotterdam and Amsterdam via Harwich ferry port.

Hopton on Sea is served by buses from Great Yarmouth, where rail connections to London can be made.

TIME TO COMPLETE

Walking:	**8 days/48 hours**
Trekking:	**5 days/39 hours**
Fastpacking:	**4 days/30 hours**
Trail running:	**3 days/23 hours**

PROS

• **Birds** – the quiet farms and grassy dunes are the perfect haven for birds, and you might spot avocets, ring ouzels, redshanks and egrets.

• **Shellfish** – some will tell you that it's the longest natural chalk ridge in the world, near Cromer and Sheringham, that makes Norfolk's crabs and lobsters taste sweeter than other British shellfish.

• **Sandy beaches** – Norfolk's long, golden beaches, soft with sand, are some of England's prettiest. Its Blue Flag Beaches offer excellent summer swimming, and are often surprisingly quiet.

CONS

• **Flat** – North Norfolk is flat, and the cliffs barely rise above the sea (consequently the coast has often been subject to flooding). This is not the trail for you is you like challenging climbs and hilltop views.

• **Roads** – particularly on the Peddars Way section, you often find yourself on (quiet country) roads rather than footpaths or bridleways.

• **Backtracking** – The Peddars Way reaches the coast at Holme next the Sea, and there is an out-and-back to the start of the Norfolk Coast Path at Hunstanton.

GOOD TO KNOW

There are five stone Norfolk Songline sculptures along the Peddars Way, a collaboration between artist Liz McGowan, storyteller Hugh Lupton and singer Helen Chadwick. The concept was inspired by Aboriginal songlines, epic songs that tell the story of a landscape.

FURTHER INFORMATION

www.nationaltrail.co.uk/en_GB/trails/peddars-way-and-norfolk-coast-path

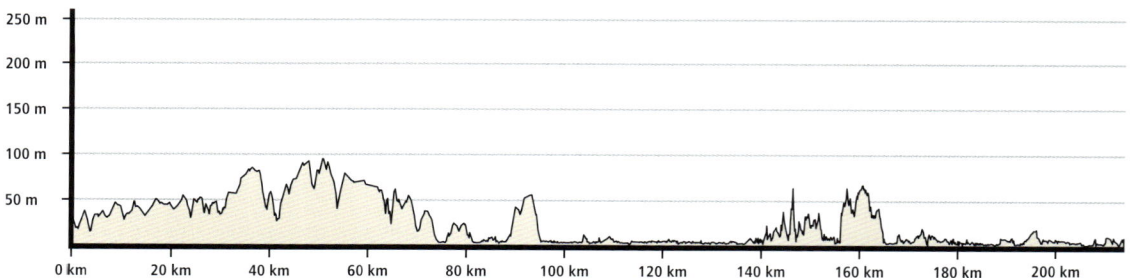

JAN	FEB	MAR	APR	MAY	JUN	JUL	AUG	SEP	OCT	NOV	DEC

North Sea

Brancaster Bay
Scolt Head Island
Holkham Bay
Blakeney Point
Cley next the Sea

Holme-next-the-Sea
Burnham Deepdale
Wells-next-the-Sea
Morston
Sheringham
Cromer
Overstrand

Hunstanton
Ringstead
Fring
Mundesley
Walcott
Eccles on Sea
North Walsham
Waxham
Stalham

Norfolk Coast AONB

A149

Fakenham
Aylsham
Hemsby

A148

River Bure
A140

A1065

Caister-on-Sea

Lynn

Castle Acre
Dereham
River Wensum
Norwich
Acle
Great Yarmouth

South Acre
A47
The Broads

Swaffham
North Pickenham
Hingham
Wymondham
Hopton on Sea

am et
A134
South Pickenham
Watton
Loddon
Lowestoft

River Wissey
Threxton
Attleborough
Long Stratton
Beccles

Stonebridge
A11
Bungay

Brandon
Harleston
A144

Thetford
Diss
River Waveney
Shadwell
S Knettishall Heath
Halesworth
Southwold

A1101
A143
Suffolk Coast & Heaths AONB

Mildenham
Eye

ENGLAND
A140
A1120
Saxmundham

market
A14
Framlingham

N
Bury St Edmunds
Aldeburgh

Stowmarket
Woodbridge

Needham Market

Haverhill
Clare
Ipswich

0   20 Kilometres

17 PENNINE WAY — 411km

The Pennine Way, a 411-kilometre route that follows the high ridge of the Pennines up the spine of Northern England, was the brainchild of Tom Stephenson, one of the early champions of walkers' rights in England. As Britain's oldest National Trail, the Pennine Way has perhaps captured walkers' imaginations as no other British trail has, and is a lifetime ambition for most walkers. The path takes you through beautiful dales, over the top of some of England's highest peaks, past waterfalls and Roman ruins. Although much of the route is now flagstoned, no walker completely escapes the bog.

The route starts in the Peak District village of Edale and begins as it goes on – with a challenging climb up Jacob's Ladder on to the Kinder Plateau. The Peak District was the first national park established in the UK, and the mass trespass over Kinder Scout in 1932 did much to bring the issue of the right to roam into public discussion. Ewan MacColl, a mass trespasser himself, wrote 'The Manchester Rambler' as a tribute to Kinder and its surroundings. Although much despised by some walkers, the flagstones have enabled the restoration of the plateau which was once a barren black bogscape – the delicate moorland is now green with cotton-grass. Over green and golden moors, the path continues, skirting the World War II aircraft wrecks at Bleaklow.

At Windy Hill, a narrow, quivering bridge carries you high above the M62 towards Brontë country. On a soaring ridge above Hebden Bridge, you approach Stoodley Pike, a monument to Napoleon's defeat that collapsed in 1854 and had to be restored. The route passes Top Withens, a crumbling farmhouse, guarded by a solitary tree, said to be the inspiration for Emily Brontë's *Wuthering Heights*.

Gargrave, a village with excellent tearooms, marks the route's entry into the Yorkshire Dales. The route meanders along the River Aire until it reaches the towering cliff of Malham Cove. You face a short, sharp climb up to the eerie, slippery limestone pavement. After Malham Tarn, another challenging peak appears on the horizon – the route diverts up to the exposed summit of Pen-y-Ghent, one of the Yorkshire Three Peaks. Past Horton in Ribblesdale, an elongated village bounded by a pub at each end, you glimpse the long sweep of the Ribblehead Viaduct.

Hawes is an attractive market town and home to Wensley-dale cheese. In the back garden of a pub just outside Hawes is Hardraw Force, England's largest single-drop waterfall. A long, hard pull over Great Shunner Fell leads you into the prettiest of the Yorkshire Dales, Swaledale. Near Keld, you can sit on a stone in the stream, cooling your blistered feet in the sparkling cascades.

The Tan Hill Inn is the highest pub in Britain and is frequently snowed in – New Year's revellers were stranded for three days in 2010. The pub marks the boundary between the Yorkshire Dales and the North Pennines. You should enjoy pulling on your dry boots, smoked warm in front of the fire, because the next section is one of the boggiest en route. At God's Bridge the route passes under the A66 and this inauspicious subway marks the halfway point of the Pennine Way. There is a sign marking this achievement – on the bottom of it, someone has scrawled 'Suckers'.

◀ RUNNING ALONG THE PENNINE WAY BELOW THE SOUTHERN SLOPES OF PEN-Y-GHENT, YORKSHIRE DALES. © JEN & SIM BENSON

TOP WITHENS, OR WUTHERING HEIGHTS, NEAR HAWORTH. © ALEX RODDIE

After Middleton in Teesdale, there is an easy pleasant stretch along the River Tees, passing Low Force, High Force and Cauldron Snout. You'll be rewarded for a tedious marshy trek up Maize Beck by the sudden panorama from the top of High Cup Nick where the ground disappears in front of your feet.

After Dufton, you'll climb up towards the golfball radar station that never seems to get any closer. If the Helm Wind isn't blowing, it's a fine ridge walk with the gentle farmlands of the Eden Valley to one side and the bleak North Pennine moors to the other, a reminder of how the Pennine Ridge divides the country. On a clear day, you'll see an impressive silhouette of the Lake District peaks to the west. Cross Fell is the highest point in England outside of the Lake District and walkers are often grateful for the shelter offered by Greg's Hut, a bothy just below the peak.

Past Alston, the highest market town in England, some walkers take the railway trail but the purists follow the original route as it curves up and down the hillside opposite. After Greenhead, the path climbs to Hadrian's Wall.

The next eighteen kilometres of the route takes in some of the best sections of the wall and, midway through this section, you can pause at the town of Once Brewed, just beneath the wall, and lunch at the YHA's flagship hostel, The Sill.

The quietness of the final section – after the popular Hadrian's Wall section – will be a shock. The path passes some of the seldom-walked Northumberland hills, passing The Cheviot (Northumberland's highest point). Past reservoirs and vast conifer forests, more bog, and the charmingly named Shitlington Crags – the Pennine Way is replete with rude place names to divert the tired rambler – the route across the Scottish border is desolate and high, and feels very different to the greener farmland and rolling dales of the first half. A long road descends into Kirk Yetholm, and the welcome walls of the Border Hotel, which mark the finish.

Edale is easily reached by train from Manchester (with its international airport) or Sheffield. Travel to and from Kirk Yetholm is more convoluted, involving buses to Kelso, and then onwards. There are several youth hostels on

LOOKING DOWN ON THE PENNINE WAY FROM MALHAM'S LIMESTONE PAVEMENT.
© JOHN COEFIELD

the route, and ample bed and breakfast providers and campsites. On most days, you can end your walk somewhere with a cosy pub or two. The non-camper faces issues on the first and last day – there is little en route for the first sixty-five kilometres (until Brontë country is reached). Also, if you're not wild camping, the last forty-five kilometres must be tackled in one go, or pickups from an isolated road must be arranged.

Every year, a hardy bunch of ultrarunners set off in January to attempt to run the Pennine Way in seven days. Most walkers prefer to take two or three weeks, and set off later in the year – even in April, the higher sections may be covered in snow; mist, rain and blustery winds are a hazard at all times of year.

Alfred Wainwright, the great Lake District fellwalker and writer, offered to buy anyone who completed the Pennine Way half a pint, and tired hikers still get their free drink in the Border Hotel at Kirk Yetholm (or the Old Nags Head in Edale for those walking north to south).

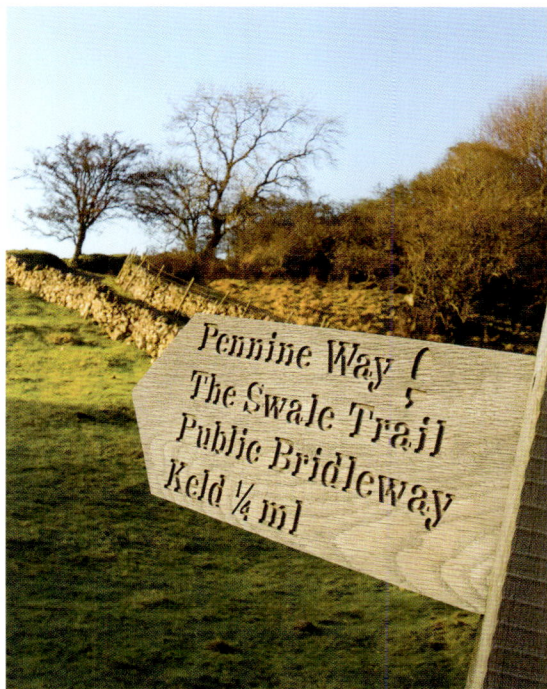

MODERN SIGNAGE IN THE YORKSHIRE DALES. © JOHN COEFIELD

17 PENNINE WAY: ESSENTIAL INFORMATION

TRAIL ESSENTIALS

Start:	**Edale, Derbyshire, England**
End:	**Kirk Yetholm, Scottish borders, Scotland**
Distance:	**411km**
Ascent/descent:	**9,870m/10,010m**

HOW TO GET THERE

Edale has direct rail connections to Sheffield, Manchester, and Manchester Airport.

Kirk Yetholm has bus connections to Kelso. From Kelso, bus connections are available to Newcastle upon Tyne, Edinburgh and Berwick-upon-Tweed.

TIME TO COMPLETE

Walking:	**21 days/128 hours**
Trekking:	**13 days/104 hours**
Fastpacking:	**10 days/78 hours**
Trail running:	**7 days/56 hours**

PROS

• **Iconic British views** – from the sparkling waterfall at Kinder Downfall, the unearthly limestone pavement at Malham Cove, via High Cup Nick, Britain's Grand Canyon, and Cross Fell, one of England's highest peaks, to the sycamore tree standing in the dip of Hadrian's Wall.

• **Tearooms** – the long southern stretch through the Yorkshire Dales passes market towns and villages with plenty of cosy cafes.

• **Bogs** – whether it's at Bleaklow or Sleightholme Moor, or fording Jenkins Burn, no walker escapes the skin-rejuvenating effects of a dip in the Way's infamous black bogs.

CONS

• **Crowds** – the Pennine Way is one of Britain's best-known long-distance trails, and some sections, such as Malham Cove, are also very popular with day-trippers.

• **Long days** – because towns and villages are strung out along the route, you'll often face the prospect of walking thirty kilometres or more in a day.

• **Weather** – the Pennines are one of the wettest regions in the UK, so expect plenty of rain that may turn to snow in the winter.

GOOD TO KNOW

In 2019, Jasmin Paris smashed the overall Spine Race course record by more than twelve hours, when she completed the Pennine Way in eighty-three hours and twelve minutes. Mike Hartley held the record for fastest known time for thirty one years, until John Kelly beat it by just thirty-four minutes in July 2020. Kelly held the record for just eight days, as Damian Hall shaved nearly three hours off to set a new fastest time of two days, sixteen hours and forty-six minutes on 24 July 2020.

FURTHER INFORMATION

The Pennine Way (Cicerone, 2017); *Pennine Way: Official National Trail Guide* (Aurum, 2016). Numerous personal accounts of walking the Way are also available (Simon Armitage, Mark Wallington, Mark Richards). *www.nationaltrail.co.uk/en_GB/trails/pennine-way*

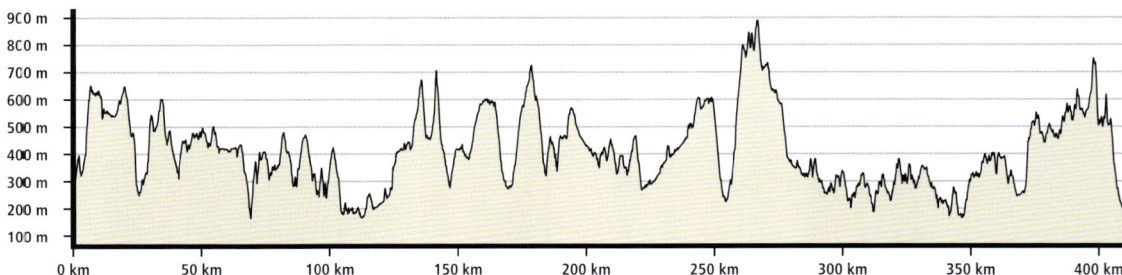

JAN	FEB	MAR	APR	MAY	JUN	JUL	AUG	SEP	OCT	NOV	DEC

SCOTLAND
ENGLAND
North Sea
Solway Firth
Morecambe Bay
The Pennines
Biggar
Innerleithen
Melrose
Kelso
Coldstream
Kirk Yetholm
Wooler
Selkirk
The Cheviot
Jedburgh
Cheviot Hills
Alnwick
Hawick
Moffat
Byrness
Northumberland National Park
Langholm
Kielder Water
Bellingham
Dumfries
Corbridge
Newcastle upon Tyne
Brampton
Haltwhistle
Carlisle
Slaggyford
Sunderland
Alston
North Pennines AONB
Durham
Cross Fell
Great Dun Fell
Penrith
Keswick
Dufton
High Cup Nick
Middleton-in-Teesdale
Middlesbrough
Barnard Castle
Appleby-in-Westmorland
Darlington
Lake District National Park
Ambleside
Kirkby Stephen
North York Moors National Park
Windermere
Kendal
Hawes
Yorkshire Dales National Park
Thirsk
Barrow-in-Furness
Horton in Ribblesdale
Pen-y-Ghent
Settle
Lancaster
Forest of Bowland AONB
Gargrave
Skipton
Harrogate
York
Keighley
Blackpool
Bradford
Leeds
Burnley
Preston
Blackburn
Hebden Bridge
Huddersfield
Wakefield
Rochdale
Bolton
Marsden
Doncaster
Manchester
Bleaklow Head
Liverpool
Glossop
Sheffield
Kinder Scout
Edale
Peak District National Park
Macclesfield
Buxton
Chester
0
20 Kilometres
N
M74
A697
A68
A1
A697
A7
A696
A68
A74(M)
A69
A1
A595
M6
A66
A66
A19
A1(M)
A595
A19
A59
M6
A629
M55
M65
A646
M62
M62
M61
M1
M18
A628
M62
M56
M6
A515
M1

18 RAAD NY FOILLAN – 157km

Douglas

In the 1930s, the Isle of Man attracted half a million tourists a year, largely Lancashire workers flocking to what John Betjeman described as the 'Naples of the North'. The ferries are quieter now, and you may have long sections of the 157-kilometre Raad ny Foillan (The Way of the Gull) to yourself, save for the gannets and the sheep. But the attractions that once drew the hordes to the island remain – a warm welcome, a slower, gentler pace of life, a temperate climate and horse-drawn trams along the promenade at Douglas. The coastal path will take you through towns and fishing harbours, along high exposed cliffs and sandy beaches, past lighthouses and castles.

You can step right on to the route from the ferry (or, indeed, the airport). The trail starts at Douglas Harbour and climbs out of the town, past the eleven-mirrored Victorian camera obscura where, in the summer, you can spy on fellow tourists. Although the route is on a road, this is Marine Drive, once the route of the tramway and opened as a coastal road in 1962 – frequent rockslides made it too expensive to maintain so it is closed to through traffic now. The castellated gate at the start of the drive was intended as a tollhouse.

Past the abandoned resort of Port Soderick, the road is swapped for a high, narrow cliff path with spectacular views. The route passes the island's airport, Ronaldsway, just before the island's old capital of Castletown, with its medieval Castle Rushen. A low grassy route along the shore takes you to Port St Mary, once an important fishing village. After a gentle climb to the rocky fissures of the Chasms, you will get a glimpse of the Calf of Man, the island's baby neighbour across the Sound.

The picturesque resort town of Port Erin marks the start of your journey along the western coast. Leaving Port Erin, the route climbs up Bradda Hill, makes a steep descent to Fleshwick Bay, steeply ascends to Lhiatte ny Beinee and falls away again before climbing one final time to the summit of Cronk ny Arrey Laa, the highest point en route (437 metres). This heathered coast was once mining country. There is a cafe at the secluded beauty spot of Niarbyl, 'the tail'.

The route takes you past the bosky gorge of Glen Maye and then over ferny cliffs to reach the fishing port of Peel. If you stop overnight, you should have a kipper for breakfast – Moore's Kipper Yard is the last traditional curing yard on the island. Peel Castle, a Viking castle built for King Magnus Barefoot, stands on an island, connected to the town by a causeway. Peel was once the Norse capital of the island.

After Peel, the route veers slightly inland, following the route of the old Manx Northern Railway, now a wide grassy path. At Glen Mooar, the missing viaduct forces you down to the beach to reach the village of Kirk Michael, with its Norse crosses. The beach section past Orrisdale Head is tidal – at high tide, you must return to the railway. Near Jurby, you take an energy-sapping route across sand and shingle beaches, although there are easier paths inland should you prefer.

◀ SIGNPOST SOUTH OF FLESHWICK BAY.
© CLAIRE MAXTED/WILD GINGER RUNNNG

The stream of Lhen Trench must be waded across before you reach the red and white lighthouse at the Point of Ayre, the island's most northerly point. The lighthouse here, the island's oldest, was built by Robert Stevenson (grandfather of the novelist Robert Louis Stevenson). The route to Ramsey, now heading south down the island's east coast, continues along the beach and may be impassable at high tide. Ramsey, the island's second largest town, is a hotspot for traditional folk music, and holds an annual Celtic music festival.

The route follows the road, offering plenty of opportunities to spot the trams of the Manx Electric Railway. A coastal route soon leaves the road, but you may be forced back on to the road at Port e Vullen at high tide. In spring, the green cliffs of Maughold Brooghs are strewn with bluebells and gorse. Another lighthouse stands tall on Maughold Head – it was designed by the grandsons of Robert Stevenson, cousins of Robert Louis Stevenson.

You follow quiet country roads into Laxey, where you will want to admire Lady Isabella on the hillside; the twenty-two-metre-wide water wheel is the largest working water wheel in the world, used to pump water from the Great Laxey Mine. Should you want to climb Snaefell, the island's highest point and only mountain (621 metres), Laxey is a good starting point. Although you might prefer to board the mountain railway to the peak – you can even book a special sunset summit dining trip.

At the end of the beach, a ferny path leads to the quiet cove of Garwick Bay, its name meaning 'pleasant bay'. You then rejoin the route of the Manx Electric Railway to return to Douglas, where the Tower of Refuge stands proud in the harbour. It was built on St Mary's Isle to offer shelter to shipwrecked mariners, who often found themselves wrecked on this rock.

PORT SODERICK BEACH, NORTH-EAST OF CASTLETOWN. © CLAIRE MAXTED/WILD GINGER RUNNNG

The good public transport provision, with convenient explorer tickets, means it is straightforward to base yourself in one town for the trip. Bus services are infrequent to the Point of Ayre, so if you are relying on public transport, it is worth considering completing the Jurby to Ramsey section (twenty-three kilometres) in one day. At Ramsey, you can catch the Manx Electric Railway back into Douglas (and you may be lucky enough to get a seat in one of the original Victorian carriages). Steam trains run from Douglas to Port Erin and bus services undertake a circuit of most of the island.

The route may be walked at any time of year, but between November and March public transport is much more limited. You should avoid your visit coinciding with TT Races (or other motorsports events), when accommodation will be almost impossible to find and up to 50,000 spectators flood the island every day. The island is not part of the United Kingdom (it is a crown dependency) or a full member of the EU. It has its own money and postage stamps, although British currency is generally accepted.

Few people have discovered the joys of the Raad ny Foillan. While there are some road sections, and some strenuous beach sections, the gorse and fern paths across cliffs, the dramatic stone cliffs and the pretty villages and historic castles more than make up for that. The island's culture and history is unique, a mixture of Celtic and Norse, never quite English; the islanders are fiercely proud of their independence. It is said that from the summit of Snaefell you can see six countries – Man itself, England, Wales, Scotland, Ireland and Heaven. Heaven might be walking the pretty cliff paths of the island, with the sun on your back, and only cormorants for company.

SPANISH HEAD, SOUTH-WEST OF THE CHASMS, ON THE WAY TO THE CALF OF MAN. © CLAIRE MAXTED/WILD GINGER RUNNNG

18 RAAD NY FOILLAN: ESSENTIAL INFORMATION

TRAIL ESSENTIALS

Start:	**Douglas, Isle of Man**
End:	**Douglas, Isle of Man**
Distance:	**157km**
Ascent/descent:	**2,840m/2,840m**
Also known as:	**The Way of the Gull; Isle of Man Coastal Path**

HOW TO GET THERE

Douglas has ferries from Liverpool, Belfast, Dublin, Birkenhead and Heysham – the closest international airport is Liverpool. The island's airport, Ronaldsway, is on the route and offers flights to UK mainland airports.

TIME TO COMPLETE

Walking:	**7 days/44 hours**
Trekking:	**5 days/36 hours**
Fastpacking:	**4 days/27 hours**
Trail running:	**3 days/20 hours**

PROS

• **Stargazing** – its remote location and few urban settlements make the Isle of Man an excellent place to stargaze. It has twenty-six Dark Sky Discovery Sites, and you might even be able to see the Northern Lights from its northern shores.

• **Vintage railways** – the Manx Electric Railway between Douglas and Ramsey is the longest narrow-gauge railway in the British Isles (twenty-seven kilometres) and two of the three carriages that opened on the route in 1893 are still in use. The mountain railway to the summit of Snaefell, which connects with the Manx Electric Railway at Laxey, is Britain's only electric mountain railway. The Isle of Man Steam Railway, connecting Douglas and Port Erin, also uses original stock from its opening in 1873. And if three unique railways are enough, you can enjoy a ride in the horse-drawn trams that have been pulled along Douglas's seafront since 1876.

• **Castles** – the trail passes Peel Castle, Derby Fort and Castle Rushen as well as the earthwork remains of a fort, Cronk Howe Mooar.

CONS

• **Roads** – there are significant sections along tarmac roads, but unless you mistime your visit to coincide with the TT Races you should not encounter too much traffic.

• **Tidal sections** – some sections of the route are not passable at high tide, which means you must check the tide tables before setting off, and may find yourself diverted along even more road sections.

GOOD TO KNOW

As you walk along the Promenade at Douglas, look out for a new statue – the council plans to erect a tribute to island natives, the Bee Gees, who were born and grew up on the island before emigrating to Australia. Other famous locals include Kush, the red panda, who has escaped not once but twice from the island's wildlife park – he was safely recaptured after his latest escape in January 2020.

FURTHER INFORMATION

www.visitisleofman.com;
The Isle of Man Coastal Path (Cicerone, 2004).

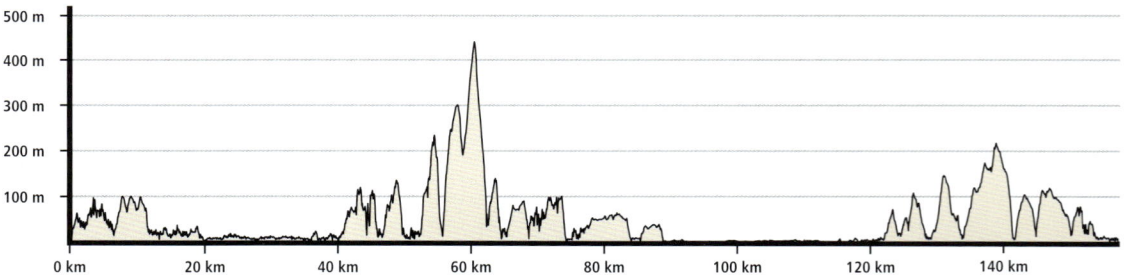

JAN	FEB	MAR	APR	MAY	JUN	JUL	AUG	SEP	OCT	NOV	DEC

Point of Ayre

Cranstal

A16

Andreas

Jurby

A10

Regaby

A10

Irish Sea

Ramsey
Bay

Ballaugh

Sulby

Lezayre

Ramsey

Orrisdale
A3

Glen Auldyn

Maughold

Kirk Michael

A14

North Barrule

Dreemskerry

A2

Slieau Freoaghane

Snaefell

Clagh Ouyr

Sartfell

Isle of Man

Beinn y Phott

Bulgham Bay

Peel

Colden

A18

Laxey

Laxey Bay

Patrick

St Johns

Slieau Ruy

B12

Baldrine

Garwick Bay

Glen Maye

Crosby

Foxdale

A1

Glen Vine

Strang

Onchan

A24

Niarbyl Bay

A27

Douglas Bay

Douglas

Cronk ny Arrey Laa

A25

Crogga

Douglas Head

Irish Sea

Bradda Hill

Colby

Ballasalla

Port Erin Bay

Port Erin

Strandhall

Port St Mary

Castletown

Derby Haven

Perwick Bay

Castletown
Bay

Port Bravag

Martha Gullet

Spanish Head

alf of Man

N

0   5 Kilometres

19 SOUTH DOWNS WAY – 162km

The 162-kilometre South Downs Way leads you from Winchester to Eastbourne, across the rolling, green South Downs and past villages that have stood still in time. On these sunny hills, the Way is never flat but never steep. Saving its best until last, you'll reach the shining sea, and walk the high white cliffs of the Seven Sisters, arguably more stunning than Dover's famous cliffs.

The trail begins in the historic city of Winchester where you might like to make time to visit Jane Austen's grave in the Gothic cathedral or view (a medieval replica of) King Arthur's legendary Round Table in the Great Hall (all that remains of the city's castle). The South Downs Way starts at the City Mill – until 2005 it was a YHA hostel, one of the earliest to be opened. Hostellers used to jump, clinging to a rope for 'safety', into the River Itchen to wash.

You follow the river down to the ruins of the bishops' palace of Wolvesey Castle, testament to the wealth and power of the bishops of Winchester. Mary I, Bloody Mary, married Philip of Spain at Winchester in 1554, and they held their wedding reception under a gold-threaded cloth of state in the east hall of Wolvesey Castle.

After crossing high above the M3 motorway and busy A31, you'll enter the South Downs National Park, Britain's newest National Park (created in 2011). The first section of the Way passes through farmland – poppied wheat fields and golden waves of rapeseed. In spring, the wide trail, passing under the arches of beech trees, will twinkle with primroses, bluebells and daffodils. South of the village of Chilcomb, the tranquillity may be shattered by the sound of gunfire on the Ministry of Defence's rifle range. The military associations continue at Cheesefoot Head, a natural amphitheatre, where General Eisenhower addressed the American troops before D-Day. The area is now home to the Boomtown festival; the South Downs Way is diverted around the festival site in August.

Beacon Hill, home to a trig point, is one of the first climbs en route. Old Winchester Hill is topped with an Iron Age fort – in addition to stunning views, possibly even of the Isle of Wight, you might be lucky enough to glimpse meadow brown or chalkhill blue butterflies here in the summer.

Butser Hill (271 metres) is the highest point on the South Downs ridge, and the highest point on the trail – although the hills on the Way are never particularly steep or high, the trail is extremely undulating. In spring, you may be treated to a fine display of aerial acrobatics by pairs of skylarks. The beech woods of Queen Elizabeth Country Park are home to deer, foxes and stoats.

The route passes the eighteenth-century folly, the Vandalian Tower, often called Lady Hamilton's Folly, because Hamilton, Nelson's mistress, would drive her carriage there to watch for her lover's returning ships. The high vantage point of Harting Down gives panoramic views over the steepled villages of the South Downs. The Way officially skirts around the second Beacon Hill, but many choose to take a shortcut over the summit.

◀ THE GENTLY UNDULATING, CHALKY SOUTH DOWNS WAY.
© DEIRDRE HUSTON

BEACHY HEAD LIGHTHOUSE. © DEIRDRE HUSTON

The Devil's Jumps are five large bell barrows – on Midsummer's Day, they are aligned with the setting sun. Amberley, the halfway point of the Way, is one of the prettiest villages in the South Downs, and conveniently has a railway station. Chanctonbury Ring is a hilltop fort, and may also be a handy lunch stop – allegedly if you run seven times anticlockwise around the fort, the devil will appear and offer you a bowl of soup in exchange for your soul. The South Downs obviously kept the devil well occupied, because you'll soon be at the deep valley of the Devil's Dyke, now a popular gliding spot. The main menace now, however, is not Beelzebub, but cows – there have been several incidents with cattle on this section of path.

Atop of a windy hill near Clayton, the two white windmills, Jack and Jill, stand proud. Jill is a working flour mill, lovingly restored by volunteers, even after she caught fire in 1987 when the Great Storm turned her sails against the brakes. There is normally an ice cream van in the car park at the top of the stiff climb up Ditchling Beacon.

The South Downs Way is bridleway for most of its length, but at Alfriston the footpath and bridleway diverge. You should follow the bridleway if you want to see the Long Man of Wilmington. The inland route also takes you through Jevington, the village where banoffee pie was invented at the Hungry Monk restaurant (now holiday cottages) in 1971.

The footpath leads to the cliffs, but first walkers are rewarded with their own chalk carving, the White Horse at Litlington, carved into the hillside in 1924 on the site of an older carving. After the geography-textbook oxbow lakes of the Cuckmere Estuary, you reach the coast at the Seven Sisters, a gleaming white chalk cliff which is always crumbling; it shines beneath you as you walk the grassy peaks and troughs of this most beautiful section of British coastline.

At Beachy Head, the highest chalk sea cliff in Britain, you can look down on the red and white lighthouse – built in 1902, this was the last offshore lighthouse to be built by Trinity House. It was a replacement for the clifftop light-house, Belle Tout. Belle Tout had to be moved in 1999

THE SOUTH DOWNS WAY NEAR TOTTINGTON. © DEIRDRE HUSTON

when its foundations became unstable because of cliff movements. It is now a luxury bed and breakfast if you want somewhere spectacular to stay at the end of your walk. The route ends somewhat inauspiciously at an ice cream kiosk on the outskirts of Eastbourne, just off Duke's Drive – most people continue another three kilometres to the unofficial end at Eastbourne's Victorian pleasure pier where you can enjoy fish and chips.

Because the trail follows the ridge, it's usually necessary to leave the path to find accommodation, largely bed and breakfasts in the small South Downs towns and villages. There are very few facilities en route, although you will pass the occasional pub or cafe. Water taps on the trail may be turned off during the colder winter months. South Downs and Truleigh Hill are the only YHA hostels on the route (although there is also a YHA hostel in Eastbourne). As in the rest of England, wild camping is illegal without the permission of the landowner but there are campsites close to the route. More unusual accommodation options en route include the yurts at the Sustainability Centre near Petersfield and the lighthouse near Beachy Head.

The route can be walked at any time of year although, as it is predominantly a ridge walk, you are exposed in heavy rain or ferocious sunshine. The Way is popular with cyclists and horse riders, as well as walkers, and is perhaps best avoided in the summer months. As a bridleway, the trail is generally wide and hard-surfaced, although chalk-topped sections may be slippery in rain.

The route may be walked from sea to city, or city to sea. But there is something to be said for turning your back on the city and walking into the quiet green beauty of the Downs. And walking until the ground disappears beneath your feet and there is no further for you to go.

19 SOUTH DOWNS WAY: ESSENTIAL INFORMATION

TRAIL ESSENTIALS

Start: **Winchester, Hampshire, England**
End: **Eastbourne, East Sussex, England**
Distance: **162km**
Ascent/descent: **3,230m/3,240m**

HOW TO GET THERE

Winchester has a direct rail connection to London (approximately one hour) where connections may be made to London's airports, or to national and international train services.

Eastbourne has direct rail connections to London Gatwick Airport, and to London, where rail and air connections may be made.

TIME TO COMPLETE

Walking: **8 days/47 hours**
Trekking: **5 days/39 hours**
Fastpacking: **4 days/29 hours**
Trail running: **3 days/21 hours**

PROS

- **White cliffs** – the white cliffs of Seven Sisters are as iconic, and arguably more unspoilt, than Dover's. The green grassy heights of Beachy Head are some of Britain's finest coastal scenery.

- **Sun-drenched Downs** – the South Downs experiences more sunshine and less rain than most other areas of England. Eastbourne has some claim to the disputed title of the sunniest town in Great Britain – it does hold the record for hours of sunshine in a single month, set in July 1911.

- **Butterflies** – they love the chalk grasslands of the South Downs National Park; you might encounter the Adonis and chalkhill blues, and the rare Duke of Burgundy at Harting Down.

CONS

- **Bridleways** – much of the South Down Way is bridleway, and you'll share the path with walkers and cyclists. This has its advantages – the South Downs Way has few stiles. But the route may be busy, and is often on quiet roads or hard trails.

- **Accommodation** – the South Downs Way deliberately avoids villages and towns, so you may have to make short detours to find accommodation. The South Downs are popular, and accommodation is limited, so book in advance in summer.

GOOD TO KNOW

In 1998, owner Mark Roberts raised £250,000 to move the Belle Tout lighthouse away from the crumbling cliff edge at Beachy Head. Using hydraulic jacks, the 850-ton lighthouse, built in 1834, was slid back at an excruciatingly slow pace of approximately half a metre every two hours, until it came to rest seventeen metres further from the precipice – the moving mechanism was left in place so that it can be shifted again.

FURTHER INFORMATION

South Downs Way Guidemap (Vertebrate Publishing, 2020); *www.nationaltrail.co.uk/en_GB/trails/south-downs-way*

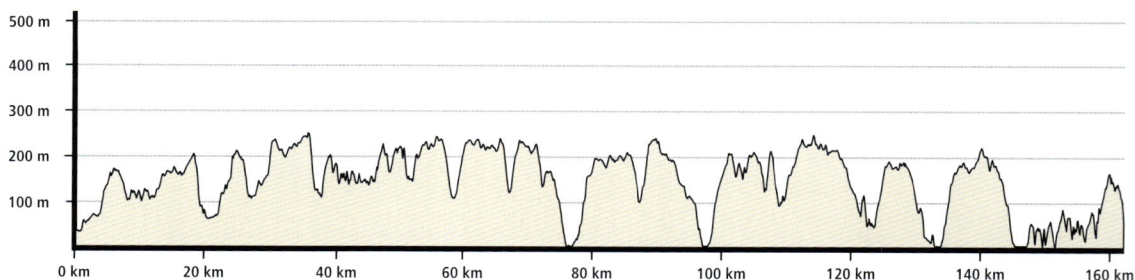

| JAN | FEB | MAR | APR | MAY | JUN | JUL | AUG | SEP | OCT | NOV | DEC |

ENGLAND

North Downs

Surrey Hills

South Downs National Park

English Channel

Eastbourne
Beachy Head
Birling Gap
Jevington
Alfriston
Seaford
Southease
Rodmell
Peacehaven
Lewes
Castle Hill
Plumpton
Ditchling Beacon
Pyecombe
Brighton
Truleigh Hill
Steyning
Henfield
Worthing
Washington
Storrington
Chantry Hill
Amberley
Houghton
Littlehampton
Kithurst Hill
Glatting Beacon
Bognor Regis
Heyshott Down
Cocking
Linch Down
Midhurst
South Harting
Chichester
Petersfield
Burton
Butser Hill
Harwood Down
Hyden Hill
Waterlooville
Exton
Beacon Hill
Portsmouth
Fareham
Bishop's Waltham
Winchester
Eastleigh
Southampton

Sevenoaks
Tonbridge
Royal Tunbridge Wells
Heathfield
Hailsham
Crowborough
Uckfield
Oxted
East Grinstead
Haywards Heath
Redhill
Crawley
Burgess Hill
Billingshurst
Horsham
Haslemere
Farnborough
Aldershot
Farnham
Alton
Basingstoke
Whitchurch
New Alresford

Isle of Wight
Cowes
Newport
Ryde
Sandown
Ventnor

20 Kilometres
0

N

S
F

20 SOUTH WEST COAST PATH
— 986km

The South West Coast Path hugs the sea, meandering for 986 kilometres along some of England's wildest and most stunning coast. You will pass pretty seaside resorts, busy fishing harbours, deep tin mines and walk around the very end of the country. This is a coast of smugglers and shipwrecks, of industrious mining and quarrying, of fishing and farming. The path passes over some of England's highest cliffs, and you'll face long days of steep climbs to stunning views, followed by knee-jarring descents to the beach, but you can reward yourself with some of England's freshest seafood or smooth ice cream from local dairies.

The South West Coast Path starts in Minehead, on the Bristol Channel, at the foot of Exmoor. From Minehead, you may follow the steep coast path along England's highest cliffs or take the gorsey, moorland path. At Porlock Weir, you'll pass a new tidal saltmarsh, created by a storm in 1996. At Culbone, with England's smallest parish church, you face another cliff path or wooded, waterfall path choice. Past Lynmouth, you'll walk the jagged Valley of the Rocks, inspiration for *Lorna Doone* and now home to feral goats, and climb over Great Hangman, the highest sea cliff in England and the highest point en route (318 metres).

The path becomes gentler as it passes the Devon resorts of Ilfracombe and Woolacombe, eventually joining the old railway tracks of the Tarka Trail towards Westward Ho!, the only British town with an exclamation mark in its name. The path passes above the historic fishing village of Clovelly, whose streets are so steep that deliveries are made by sledge. As you walk through the ancient woodland of

the Hartland Peninsula, you are now on the edge of the wild Atlantic coast and the path now zigzags over steep river valleys towards the Cornish border and Bude.

The rugged Cornish coast is the place of legends, and Arthur once held court on the grey slate cliffs of Tintagel. The small fishing village of Port Isaac is associated with a more modern character; it is home to television's *Doc Martin*. Padstow is a foody destination – Rick Stein, who also has a fish and chip shop here, opened his seafood restaurant in 1975. The dangerous, rugged coast is notorious for shipwrecks, but you are more likely to see bottlenose dolphins. The coast gets busy with caravans near the popular tourist resort of Newquay, once home to a knitting industry – the path crosses the surfers' Fistral Beach.

Near Perranporth, another popular resort, there are greater horseshoe bats in the caves. St Ives, a favourite of artists and potters, is now home to a branch of the Tate art gallery. The white lighthouse of Pendeen guides you to Cape Cornwall, England's most westerly land. This is a coastline of smugglers and miners. You'll pass the Levant Mine, famous for its 1919 disaster, and the crumbling towers of Botallack.

Past the tourist blight of Land's End, you'll pass the clifftop Minack Theatre near Porthcurno (where the first transatlantic telegraph cables came ashore). Mousehole is another postcard-pretty fishing village, famous for its

◀ ON BOLBERRY DOWN IN DEVON, OVERLOOKING SOAR MILL COVE.
© STEPHEN ROSS

TRAIL RUNNING TOWARDS SALCOMBE. © STEPHEN ROSS

stargazey pie, with pilchard heads poking out. Newlyn, another artists' favourite, is the third largest fishing harbour in Britain. You might want to stop for a refreshing dip in Penzance's newly refurbished, art deco saltwater lido, Jubilee Pool. It is a gentle, sandy stroll along the coast towards Marazion, with views of St Michael's Mount, a castled island connected to the mainland by a tidal causeway.

The Lizard, with its striking green serpentine granite, is England's most southerly point. You'll pass the circular turrets of Henry VIII's Pendennis Castle before reaching the university town of Falmouth. Past the beautiful Roseland Peninsula, the land near Mevagissey has been extensively quarried for china clay, and the resulting spoil heaps have lent the area the nickname the 'Cornish Alps'. The clay was exported from Fowey — here you catch a ferry to Polruan. This coast was Daphne du Maurier's favourite — Polridmouth provided inspiration for *Rebecca*.

Past Polperro, the wooded cliff path winds over Cornwall's highest southern cliffs, you may need to divert inland around the military firing range at Tregantle Fort to reach

the River Tamar, which marks the border with Devon. A ferry will take you to the nautical city of Plymouth — you'll walk past the city's navy and military history, particularly the Hoe on which Sir Francis Drake played bowls as the Spanish Armada advanced. Urban sprawl eventually gives way to quiet cliffs — this steep section also involves the tidal fording of the River Erme. Dolphins and seals bob in the waters off south Devon's beautiful, bluebelled cliffs as you head towards the sandy bays of Hope Cove and Salcombe, famous for its ice cream.

The pretty seaside town of Dartmouth is close to Agatha Christie's home, Greenway. Brixham is still a busy fishing port, but past it, you reach Devon's popular seaside resorts as you pass through the English Riviera. The red sandstone cliffs often stain the sea blood-red. From Teignmouth to Dawlish, the path follows one of England's most scenic railway lines, carved by Isambard Kingdom Brunel into the cliff, on the sea edge. A ferry takes you across the River Exe from Starcross to the sandy resort of Exmouth, and from there, you climb over to the cliffs, the start of the Jurassic Coast, to the long stony seafront of Budleigh Salterton. Every August, the quiet regency town of Sidmouth bustles with morris dancers, choirs and rappers at the Sidmouth Folk Festival.

Near Seaton, red cliffs give way to the shimmering white of the fossil-rich chalk cliffs – coastal erosion has caused the land here to slip into deep, wooded clefts, known as the Undercliff. The fossil town of Lyme Regis marks the border with your last county en route, Dorset. You'll pass the long pebble ridge of Chesil Beach, behind which is The Fleet, the largest tidal lagoon in Britain. The path detours inland around the lagoon, before heading back towards the Isle of Portland, famous for its quarried limestone. The path goes around the not quite island, which is linked to the mainland by Chesil Beach, before returning to Weymouth.

There is no rest for tired legs, as you pass the limestone arch of Durdle Door and climb the steep paths near Lulworth Cove. The path ends on the sandy beaches of South Haven Point, near Sandbanks.

Faced with financial devastation and homelessness, Raynor Winn and her husband Moth set off to walk the South West Coast Path, wild camping on the way. Her account of this life-changing adventure, *The Salt Path* was shortlisted for the Wainwright Prize. The South West Coast Path is Britain's most challenging National Trail, but all who embark on it, whether all in one go or in summer holidays and long weekends, will experience the joy of leaving the busy resorts behind you and discovering some of England's most beautiful coast and stunning sea views.

VIEWS ACROSS BANTHAM BEACH. © STEPHEN ROSS

20 SOUTH WEST COAST PATH: ESSENTIAL INFORMATION

TRAIL ESSENTIALS

Start: **Minehead, Somerset, England**
End: **South Haven Point, Dorset, England**
Distance: **986km**
Ascent/descent: **18,230m/18,260m**

HOW TO GET THERE

Minehead is served by buses from Taunton, the nearest railway station. Taunton has mainline rail connections to Bristol (with the nearest international airport), Birmingham and London.

South Haven Point is on edge of Poole Harbour and is served by buses running between Bournemouth and Swanage. Fast direct rail connections can be made to London (and Birmingham) from Bournemouth.

TIME TO COMPLETE

Walking: **47 days/281 hours**
Trekking: **29 days/230 hours**
Fastpacking: **22 days/172 hours**
Trail running: **16 days/126 hours**

PROS

• **Culture** – this landscape has perhaps inspired more art and literature than any other. You walk through the scenery of *Poldark*, of *Lorna Doone* and *Moonfleet*. These views have inspired Turner, Barbara Hepworth and Lamorna Birch.

• **Seafood** – From Rick Stein in Padstow, to the fishing ports of Newlyn and Brixham and Mousehole's pilchard stargazey pie, you'll have the opportunity to try some of England's freshest fish.

• **Coastal views** – from high heathered cliffs, to gorsey paths, this trail offers some of Britain's finest coastline. The sea arch at Durdle Door, the long ridge of Chesil Beach and the red sandstone cliffs on the Jurassic Coast are highlights.

CONS

• **Rivers** – they flow down to the sea through cliffs, and each of them has to be crossed – some can be waded across at the right time, some have to be bridged, some have ferries. You'll need to plan carefully to make sure each river can be crossed, particularly in winter when ferries often do not run.

• **Cliffs** – they must be climbed and descended. The red sandstone paths may be slippery when wet; the trail often follows steep stepped sections and the clifftops, particularly on the wild, boggy Cape Cornwall, can be exposed in bad weather.

• **Emmets (or ants)** – the Cornish nickname for the swarms of tourists – you'll meet them in Newquay, at the shopping centre of Land's End, at Devon's seaside resorts of Torquay and Exmouth. Devonians nickname them grockles.

GOOD TO KNOW

Most people tackle the coast path in one to two months, but Damian Hall set a new fastest time in May 2016, covering the distance in just ten days fifteen hours and eighteen minutes.

FURTHER INFORMATION

www.southwestcoastpath.org.uk

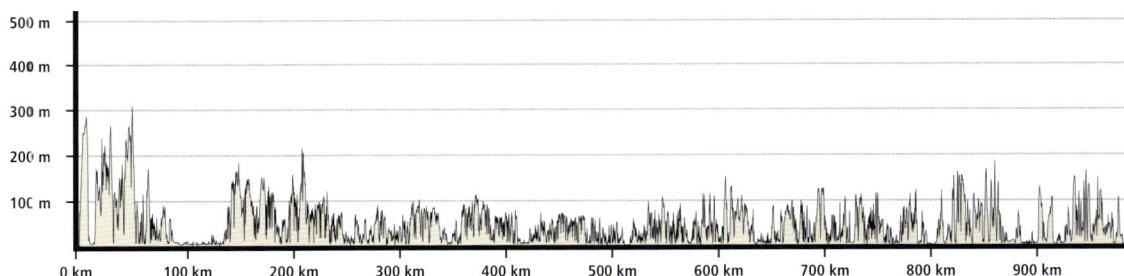

JAN	FEB	MAR	APR	MAY	JUN	JUL	AUG	SEP	OCT	NOV	DEC

Atlantic Ocean
Bristol Channel
English Channel
ENGLAND
Cardiff
Bristol
Weston-super-Mare
Bath
Chippenham
Marlborough
Wells
Warminster
Salisbury
Bridgwater
Taunton
Yeovil
Crewkerne
Honiton
Bridport
Dorchester
Bournemouth
Poole
Wareham
South Haven Point
Swanage
St Aldhelm's Head
Weymouth
Portland Bill
Lyme Bay
Lyme Regis
Seaton
Sidmouth
Exmouth
Exeter
Teignmouth
Newton Abbot
Torquay
Paignton
Brixham
Dartmouth
Stoke Fleming
Salcombe
East Prawle
Mothecombe
Stoke Point
Penlee Point
Whitsand Bay
Plymouth
Tavistock
Dartmoor National Park
North Tawton
Chulmleigh
South Molton
Exmoor National Park
Minehead
Lynton
Ilfracombe
Morte Bay
Braunton
Barnstaple
Bideford Bay
Bideford
Clovelly
Holsworthy
Bude
Lundy
Tintagel
Launceston
River Tamar
Bodmin Moor
Pentire Point
Trevose Head
Padstow
Bodmin
Liskeard
Looe
Fowey
Gribbin Head
Newquay
Ligger Point
St Agnes
Truro
Mevagissey
St Ives
Hayle
Falmouth
St Mawes
Penzance
St Just
Land's End
St Michael's Mount
Porthleven
Dolor Point
Lizard
M4
M5
A30
A350
A361
N
0
20 Kilometres

21 THAMES PATH
– 294km

Old Father Thames is England's longest river, and Britain's most important and iconic river. Perhaps that is why so many people choose to walk the UK's most popular National Trail, the 294-kilometre Thames Path. Most walk from the source (under the shadow of the Cotswolds) to the city of London, but some go against the flow. Or it might be more accurate to say that most people walk it in sections, some taking years to complete it – there are train stations dotted along the route, although west of Oxford the path is more challenging to reach.

Once infamously filthy – the Great Stink forced MPs to flee Parliament in 1858 – the Thames is now the cleanest river in the world to flow through a major city. You might want to bring a swimming costume with you, and cool off after a long day's walk with a dip in the river. You are not permitted to swim in the busy city section downstream of Putney Bridge, but the Marble Hill bathing steps at Richmond are a popular spot for urban swimmers. Out of London, you might choose to float amongst swans near Henley-on-Thames or drift under the willows at the natural pool scooped out at Buscot Weir.

The Thames springs to life, or rather, on a very wet day, muddily gurgles to the surface in an unprepossessing field in Gloucestershire. Most of the time, the only indication of the river will be the marker stone that also marks the start of the trail. For the first four or five kilometres, there is no sign of the river other than a dry ditch and a stone bridge that spans nothing more than grass. Puddles appear, and trickle together, until a stream appears and, by the time you reach Ashton Keynes, you'll be on the bank of a small river.

At St John's Lock, you reach the navigable limit of the river and a statue of Old Father Thames stands guard. Shortly after, you'll pass the perfect (and very popular) swimming spot at Buscot. The Thames Path passes through water meadows and farmers' fields full of cows, occasionally meandering away from the riverbanks. At the misnomered Newbridge, you'll find one of the oldest bridges on the Thames. On this still quiet stretch of the river, you may see a heron.

The Trout Inn at Lower Wolvercote, a favourite haunt of the fictional Inspector Morse, marks the start of a more urban Thames. You enter Oxford by passing Port Meadow, grazing land gifted to the freeman of Oxford by Alfred the Great, which, according to legend, has never been ploughed. You pass the suburb of Jericho, home to Philip Pullman's Gyptians. Through Oxford, the path is busy with cyclists, walkers and joggers. The river flows past the city, largely out of sight of its dreaming spires.

From here, the river never again seems quite so remote – you'll often hear the rails humming in the distance as another train rushes towards London. The path skips between historic towns and villages, with plenty of riverside pubs. At Henley-on-Thames, the rowers reappear – this is where the (Oxford versus Cambridge) Boat Race was first held. A little further down the river, Marlow is home to Britain's only pub with two Michelin stars, The Hand and Flowers.

◄ THE RIVER THAMES AT DAYS LOCK IN OXFORDSHIRE.
© MARK RAINSLEY

You approach London through what might be thought of as the royal outskirts. Passing Eton College's grounds (where Princes William and Harry were educated), you can enjoy a fantastic view of Windsor Castle on the opposite side of the river. You'll pass Runnymede where King John was forced to accede to the demands of the barons and sign the Magna Carta, the foundation of Britain's constitution. On the outskirts of London, it is traditional to take the Shepperton Ferry to cross to the southern bank (although Walton Bridge may be used when the ferry is not running), where you'll pass Henry VIII's Hampton Court Palace, and the King's hunting grounds at Richmond.

From Teddington, you can choose which side of the river to walk on. On the northern bank, you can stroll through Syon Park, look across the river to the grandiose art deco façade of the decommissioned Battersea Power Station, and follow the always busy Thames Embankment, reclaimed from the Thames as part of Joseph Bazalgette's nineteenth-century sewerage revolution. You'll be in the shadow of Westminster and pass a fifteenth-century BC Egyptian obelisk, but the better view of the Houses of Parliament is from the southern bank.

Perhaps the best option is to switch from bank to bank, passing Richmond and Kew Gardens on the southern bank, stopping to browse second-hand books or pick up lunch at a food market at South Bank. Then you can cross to the northern bank on Millennium Bridge, the Thames' newest bridge, to walk round the walls of the Tower of London. This gives you an opportunity to follow in the footsteps of London Marathoners and cross London's most iconic bridge, Tower Bridge – if it isn't raised for a boat to pass through.

Once you reach Greenwich, who could resist the rare opportunity to pass under the Thames by foot using the Greenwich Foot Tunnel – just behind the *Cutty Sark*. Technically the northern section of the route finishes here, so you'll have to retrace your steps to the southern bank to finish the Thames Path, although there is a Thames Path extension on the north and you might choose to walk through London Docklands until you at least reach the Woolwich Foot Tunnel. The trail officially ends at the

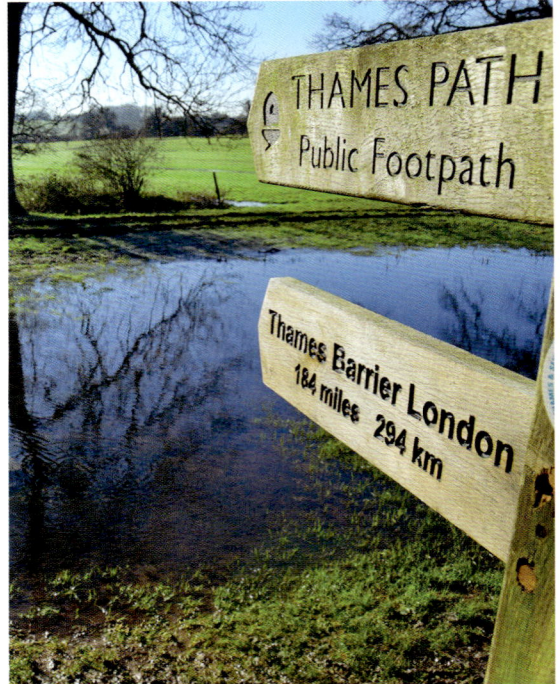

ABOVE: THE START OF THE TRAIL AT THE THAMES SOURCE. © MARK RAINSLEY
BELOW: MARSH LOCK ON THE THAMES PATH NEAR HENLEY-ON-THAMES. © JEN & SIM BENSON

Thames Barrier, although some follow the extension path further down to the estuary.

The Thames Path can be walked at any time of year although sections of the path are vulnerable to flooding, particularly in winter. It's always advisable to check the Thames Path section of the National Trail's website for updates on flooding or path diversions due to building works or maintenance.

The Thames Path is a mixture of roads and pavements, tarmac and gravel tracks and (usually muddy) towpaths. Sometimes it leaves the river to make its way through towns or across farmland. It is a level path with very little ascent or descent, and in sheltered countryside or urban areas. You're never far from the next village or town, and you can refresh yourself at any number of riverside pubs.

The closest train station to the source of the Thames is Kemble, about two kilometres from the start of the trail. The Thames Barrier can be reached on the Docklands Light Railway (Pontoon Dock). There are numerous railway stations on or near to the route, and local bus services.

Walking the Thames Path is like strolling through British history, past Windsor Castle and Hampton Court Palace, past the dreaming spires of Oxford, and Runnymede, past the Houses of Parliament and Shakespeare's Globe. But the route also takes you past docks and factories, power stations and breweries, often deserted or repurposed – but reminders that this water transported goods in and out of the city, pumped through the capital's industries, raised taxes, that the river was the liquid gold that the city was built on.

THE BUSY TIDEWAY NEAR TOWER BRIDGE. © MARK RAINSLEY

21 THAMES PATH: ESSENTIAL INFORMATION

TRAIL ESSENTIALS

Start:	**Kemble, Gloucestershire, England**
End:	**Thames Barrier, London, England**
Distance:	**294km**
Ascent/descent:	**1,010m/1,120m**

HOW TO GET THERE

Kemble is approximately two kilometres from the Thames source. Kemble offers rail connections to London, and its international airports.

Thames Barrier is served by the Pontoon Dock Station on the Docklands Light Railway, which connects with the London Underground. Charlton Station is also close by.

TIME TO COMPLETE

Walking:	**11 days/64 hours**
Trekking:	**7 days/53 hours**
Fastpacking:	**5 days/40 hours**
Trail running:	**4 days/31 hours**

PROS

• **Wild swimming** – in London you cannot swim in the Thames, without permission, between Crossness and Putney Bridge. But the rural Thames, through Buckinghamshire and beyond, offers many glorious swimming spots, especially Buscot Weir.

• **Royal history** – from castles and palaces to royal hunting grounds, and Runnymede, the site of the great compromise between the monarchy and the people, you are never far from Britain's royal history. A castle was built at Windsor by William the Conqueror, and Victoria and Albert were buried there in the Royal Mausoleum at Frogmore. The Tower of London has been castle, mint, prison and even home to the royal menagerie.

• **City sights** – the Thames Path takes you through the centre of London, past Hampton Court Palace, the Tower of London, Tower Bridge and the Houses of Parliament, to the Thames Barrier.

CONS

• **The source** – there is no sparkling spring, or altar to England's great river, at the start – often there is no sign of water at all at the source of the Thames. For the first five kilometres, the Thames is little more than a puddle that you might absent-mindedly squelch across.

• **Flooding** – certain sections of the Thames Path are very susceptible to flooding, particularly in winter and spring. There may be no alternative route other than a lengthy diversion. You should check the National Trails website for up-to-date information before embarking on your walk.

• **Urban** – near the source, the Thames Path trails through green pastures, between pretty Cotswold villages. But the path never takes you through open countryside, you are never far from the urban life and, the closer you get to London, the more built up the route is.

GOOD TO KNOW

The Thames Path is one of Britain's most popular trails, but sometimes people swim the length of the Thames. In 2011, British comedian, David Walliams, swam 225 kilometres along the Thames to raise more than £1m for charity.

FURTHER INFORMATION

www.nationaltrail.co.uk/en_GB/trails/thames-path

JAN	FEB	MAR	APR	MAY	JUN	JUL	AUG	SEP	OCT	NOV	DEC

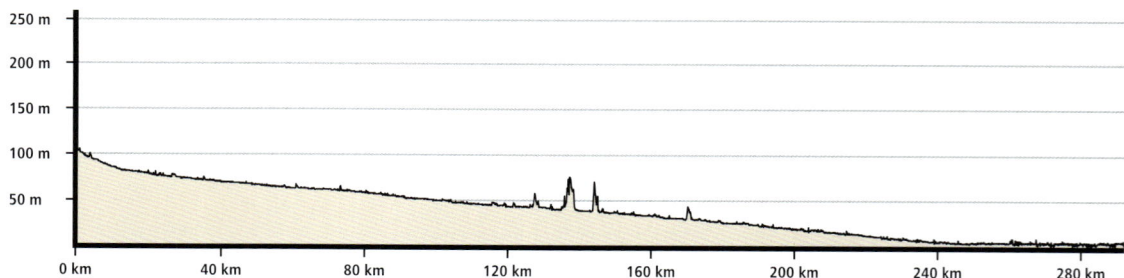

Thames Barrier
Woolwich
London
Harlow
Ware
Waltham Cross
Enfield
Edgware
Hammersmith
Brentford
Teddington
Kingston upon Thames
Croydon
Oxted
Redhill
Honley
Crawley
Horsham
Leatherhead
Surrey Hills
North Downs
Letchworth
Hitchin
Stevenage
St Albans
Watford
Uxbridge
Slough
Windsor
Egham
Woking
Guildford
Godalming
Haslemere
Milton Keynes
Leighton Buzzard
Dunstable
Luton
Hemel Hempstead
Amersham
Beaconsfield
High Wycombe
Chiltern Hills
Bourne End
Maidenhead
Bracknell
Wokingham
Farnborough
Farnham
Thames
Brackley
Bicester
Thame
Henley-on-Thames
Reading
Basingstoke
Winchester
Banbury
Oxford
Wallingford
Goring
Clifton Hampden
Didcot
Newbury
Abingdon
Swinford
Witney
Chipping Norton
Faringdon
Wantage
Ridgeway
North Wessex Downs AONB
Hungerford
Marlborough
Andover
Amesbury
Northleach
Cheltenham
Lechlade
Buscot
Cricklade
Swindon
Chippenham
Salisbury
The Cotswolds AONB
Cirencester
Kemble
Thames

M25 M1 A1(M) A10 M11 M40 M4 M3 M23 A34(T) A417 A420 A4 A429 A40

20 Kilometres
0

N

S
F

22 THE RIDGEWAY
— 140km

A small gravelled byway leads inauspiciously away from the A4 at Overton Hill, just a few miles from Avebury. This is the start of the 140-kilometre National Trail, the Ridgeway, along what is said to be Britain's oldest road. It follows the ridge of a chalk scarp, up to cross the River Thames at the Goring Gap, and then through the Chilterns to Ivinghoe Beacon. Never vertiginously high, the path is slightly elevated above the flat land around it, making it excellent for traders and armies who valued the safety such a vantage point could offer them. And now making it ideal for walkers who want wide horizons and panoramic views without breath-stealing ascents.

From the Ridgeway's start, at Overton Hill in a car park off a busy main road, a gentle green rutted path leads towards Barbury Castle. This impressive Iron Age hill fort housed American anti-aircraft guns during World War II. A high, grassy path along Smeathe's Ridge takes you past an ancient barrow and around the village of Ogbourne St George, although many choose to detour to the village pub. The Ridgeway is one of Britain's oldest routes, and it is rich in archaeological sites. The Bronze Age Liddington Castle was an inspiration to the Victorian nature writer, Richard Jefferies, Britain's Thoreau, who grew up locally.

This is a busy area of England, criss-crossed by roads, and the Ridgeway passes over the hectic M4 motorway near Swindon. Past golden fields of corn and rapeseed, you'll soon be rewarded with views of White Horse Hill, where a chalk horse has been carved into the hillside — although you'll have to leave the Ridgeway to get the best view of

the horse. The Uffington White Horse, believed to have been created 3,000 years ago, is the oldest such figure in Britain. Over the years, it has temporarily acquired a rider and dogs, thanks to the pro-hunting Countryside Alliance, and a jockey, as part of bookmaker's Paddy Power Cheltenham racing publicity.

The Neolithic chambered long barrow of Wayland's Smithy has long been a place of druidic significance, and visitors often deposit coins, although this is now discouraged. The route passes above the white horse, and past the Iron Age Uffington Castle. The Ridgeway takes a hilly path to the Devil's Punchbowl and another Iron Age hill fort, Segsbury Camp.

At Betterton Down, a tall cross stands on top of an obelisk, on a round barrow, in memorial to Baron Wantage, who was one of the founders of the British Red Cross. It is on this grassy track through Oxfordshire that you are likely to first glimpse one of the Ridgeway's red kites. The path runs briefly alongside the earthenworks Grim's Ditch. Scutchamer Knob is believed to be where Edwin of Northumbria killed Cwichelm of Wessex; it was said to be Cwichelm's burial place but excavations have found no trace of him. Though Ilsley was once famous for sheep, the Ridgeway now is more the territory of horses, the path often runs beside racetracks known as gallops — you'll find the Downlands Villages riding trails on Ilsley Downs near the A34 main road.

◀ THE RIDGEWAY NATIONAL TRAIL TOWARDS HACKPEN HILL.
© ANTHONY BURDALL/THE FRIENDS OF THE RIDGEWAY

THE RIDGEWAY CROSSING THE THAMES AT GORING AND STREATLEY. © ANTHONY BURDALL/THE FRIENDS OF THE RIDGEWAY

The route takes advantage of the disused Didcot, Newbury and Southampton Railway to reach the Thames at Goring-on-Thames (where it briefly meets the Thames Path). The route is now on the edge of the Chilterns, the wooded chalk escarpment that is an Area of Outstanding Natural Beauty. It is in the Chilterns where the successful reintro-duction of the red kites began – thirteen birds were flown over by British Airways in July 1990. It is estimated that there are now more than 10,000 red kites in Britain. The trail follows the Thames north, leaving the river just before Wallingford to cross a golf course and meet another pleasantly bluebelled section of Grim's Ditch. Near Watlington, you pass Nuffield Place, home to the founder of Morris Motors and Nuffield College, the University of Oxford's first co-educational college.

Past Watlington, the Ridgeway follows wide trails through pleasant beech woods and makes a rather less pleasant crossing of the M40 motorway. You may glimpse a steam train on the Chinnor and Princes Risborough Railway. The route passes Princes Risborough, a town that has been promoted from Monks Risborough to Earls to Princes when the manor came to be held by Edward Prince of Wales,

the brutal Black Prince. Through more Chiltern woodland, you emerge at Chequers, the country home of the British prime minister, since it was gifted to the nation in 1917. Prime Minister Boris Johnson came here to recuperate after catching COVID-19 in 2020. The footpath briefly crosses the estate before climbing to the top of Coombe Hill, with its monument to the soldiers who died in the Boer War. Every June, racers in the Coombe Hill Fell Race climb the hill, in a rare example of a southern fell race.

The trail meanders through the pleasant market town of Wendover – a market still takes place every Thursday. While some pubs have closed, Wendover still has more than its fair share. Dolly Saville, the world's oldest barmaid, worked at the Red Lion for seventy-six years until her death, aged 100, in 2015. It is estimated that she pulled more than two million pints. The route leaves Wendover through pleasant woods and arrives in Tring Park via an avenue of lime trees.

The edible dormouse is found across mainland Europe, but only found in Britain in the woods near Tring. Lionel Rothschild, a keen zoologist, kept a colony and some escaped in 1902. The Natural History Museum at Tring was his

COOMBE HILL MONUMENT ON THE RIDGEWAY NATIONAL TRAIL. © ANTHONY BURDALL/THE FRIENDS OF THE RIDGEWAY

private collection, but the Rothschilds donated it to the nation in 1937. The trail passes the railway station, a few kilometres from Tring's centre – many walkers retrace their path to here to catch the train at the end of the trail. The Ridgeway climbs to the summit of Ivinghoe Beacon, where it meets the start of the Icknield Way Path, both trails forming part of the Greater Ridgeway from Dorset to Norfolk.

The Ridgeway may be walked at any time of year, although the ancient woods of the Chilterns are particularly glorious in the autumn. However, the stony, chalky paths of the Ridgeway can be slippery in wet weather. Accommodation is limited along the route, and should be booked in advance. However, there are good public transport connections, particularly on the eastern half of the route, so it is possible to leave the trail each day. Although only legal with the permission of landowners, the official trail website notes that wild camping is often tolerated if undertaken responsibly. There are only two hostels en route.

The Ridgeway generally follows an historic route, although sometimes it chooses a more favourable path through the countryside. It is a glorious trail for the amateur archaeologist, although progress may be slow with all the ancient sites that may be visited. It picks a careful path past the busy towns of Reading, High Wycombe, Aylesbury and Oxford and yet barely seems to pass through villages. The chalk hills of the Chilterns, so close to London, are beloved by butterflies, red kites and walkers alike.

22 THE RIDGEWAY: ESSENTIAL INFORMATION

TRAIL ESSENTIALS

Start:	**Overton Hill, Wiltshire, England**
End:	**Ivinghoe Beacon, Buckinghamshire, England**
Distance:	**140km**
Ascent/descent:	**1,870m/1,790m**

HOW TO GET THERE

Overton Hill is not well served by public transport. You may park at the start, but most people choose to visit Avebury and walk to Overton from there. Avebury has buses to Pewsey (the closest railway station) and Swindon, with its busier railway station. Although Bristol is the closest international airport, London's airports are also close.

Ivinghoe Beacon is approximately five kilometres from Tring, where direct rail connections are available to London. Bus services run from Tring to the bottom of the Beacon, but many choose to retrace their route on the Ridgeway to Tring instead – the same bus also serves Dunstable, which offers onward connections to London Luton Airport.

TIME TO COMPLETE

Walking:	**6 days/36 hours**
Trekking:	**4 days/30 hours**
Fastpacking:	**3 days/23 hours**
Trail running:	**3 days/17 hours**

PROS

• **Red kites** – by the 1980s, Britain's red kite population was on the brink of extinction, with only a few dozen in Wales. The Chilterns were at the forefront of one of Britain's most successful conservation efforts as red kites were reintroduced there in 1990. Now you would be unlucky not to glimpse several as you walk the Ridgeway.

• **The Chilterns** – the high, grassy ridges, country houses and wooded slopes of the Chiltern Hills make them the prettiest countryside within easy reach of London. They are wildlife rich; you may see deer, badgers and bats.

• **Woods** – planted as source material for High Wycombe's furniture industry, the oak and beech woods of the Chilterns, with their bluebells and violets, make for pleasant, shady walking.

CONS

• **Accommodation** – there is limited accommodation en route, and you may have to add kilometres to the end of your day to find a room. There is little in the way of budget accommodation, unless you are prepared to wild camp.

• **Roads** – although the trail does not have long road sections, this area of England is criss-crossed with busy highways, and you will find yourself crossing two motorways, and several more main roads, some by bridge and tunnel, some by a well-timed crossing.

GOOD TO KNOW

As you walk along the Ridgeway near Watlington, you are following in the footsteps of Joe Rose and Clarissa Mellon, who enjoyed a walk through the Chilterns and followed parts of the Ridgeway before stopping for a picnic. They witnessed a hot air balloon being swept away, its only passenger a young child, and the death of one of the men who comes to the rescue. This is the opening scene of Ian McEwan's *Enduring Love*. McEwan, who has lived in the Chilterns, is a keen walker himself.

FURTHER INFORMATION

www.nationaltrail.co.uk/en_GB/trails/the-ridgeway; *The Ridgeway* (Cicerone, 2016).

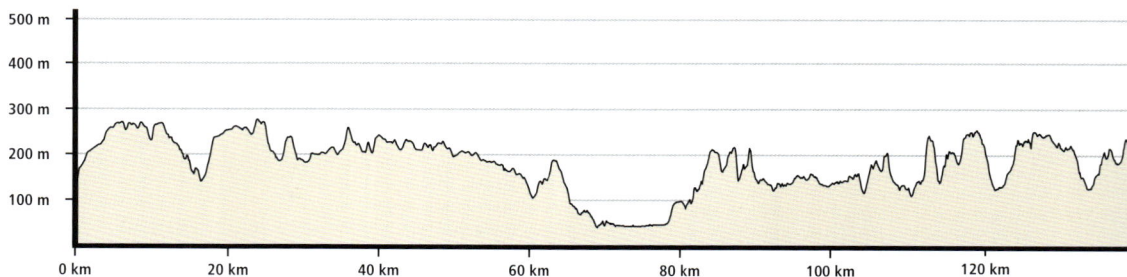

JAN	FEB	MAR	APR	MAY	JUN	JUL	AUG	SEP	OCT	NOV	DEC

Dunstable

Hemel Hempstead

Ivinghoe Beacon

Steps Hill

Tring

Wigginton

Berkhamsted

Amersham

Wendover

Coombe Hill

Aylesbury

Princes Risborough

Bledlow

Chinnor

Thame

Lewknor

Watlington

Harcourt Hill

Nuffield

North Stoke

High Wycombe

Gerrards Cross

Beaconsfield

Slough

Maidenhead

Henley-on-Thames

Reading

Windsor

Egham

Ascot

Bracknell

Cambenley

Guildford

Wokingham

Yateley

Chiltern Hills

Goring-on-Thames

River Thames

Pangbourne

Goring Gap

Wallingford

Oxford

Didcot

Abingdon

Chilton

Tadley

Basingstoke

Thatcham

Newbury

Bicester

ENGLAND

Vale of White Horse

Wantage

Letcombe Bassett

North Wessex Downs
AONB

Hungerford

Witney

Faringdon

River Thames

White Horse Hill

Charlbury Hill

Liddington Hill

Burford

Carterton

Lechlade

Ogbourne St George

Marlborough

Rough Hill

Burbage

Tidworth

Fairford

Swindon

Avebury

Overton Hill

Pewsey

Upavon

The Cotswolds
AONB

Northleach

Cricklade

N

10 Kilometres

0

DURHAM

YORK

23 WAINWRIGHT'S COAST TO COAST – 281km

Alfred Wainwright, the great Lakeland fellwalker, didn't much like the Pennine Way and thought that he could probably do better. So he devised a Coast to Coast walk, across Cumbria and Yorkshire, a 281-kilometre trek designed to take you through the very best countryside that England has to offer. Walkers must dip their boots in the sea at both start and finish, but beyond that, the choice of how to cross the country is theirs. Wainwright suggested a route and over the years signposts and maps have established something more of a trail, but the philosophy behind the Coast to Coast is that walkers should pick the paths that they want to follow. Whichever way you go, you will walk through the best of England's varied scenery, through fell and forest, along rivers and shores, through bog and moor and rock and farmland.

Most walkers traverse from west to east, partly to keep the wind and rain at their back. The start is marked, in the Cumbrian village of St Bees, by the Wainwright Wall on the beach. After wetting your feet, you follow a cliff path along the red sandstone buff of St Bees Head for nearly seven kilometres. On a clear day, you can see the coasts of Scotland, Ireland and the Isle of Man as well as the impending Lakeland fells. The St Bees Lighthouse, long automated, was the last coal-fired lighthouse in Britain until it burnt down in 1822 – to be replaced by the current incarnation.

The route soon leaves the shore, and after Cleator the climb up Dent marks your entry into the Lake District. At the top you'll be rewarded with more fine views of the lakes and the coast, all the way to Ireland, and the nuclear site at Sellafield. At Ennerdale Water, you can either scramble a tricky stony path around the south of the reservoir or follow a gentler path to the north. In the shadow of Pillar and Great Gable, you'll reach the YHA's most remote youth hostel, Black Sail.

Wainwright's original route rises above Loft Beck, but you might instead choose the variation along the rocky path up Red Pike and past High Stile and Hay Stacks. This route will take you beside Innominate Tarn, where Wainwright's ashes were scattered. Whichever route you take, a steep stone tramway leads you down to the Honister Slate Mine.

The western lakes are often quiet, difficult to reach and out of the way of most tourists. Bustling Grasmere, once home to the Wordsworths, is not, although you can reward yourself with a slab of the town's famous gingerbread. You'll follow in the footsteps of the Wordsworths, to climb up to Grisedale Tarn, where you can either head down the beckside directly to Patterdale or climb up Helvellyn, England's third highest peak, before following the arête down.

If you don't climb Helvellyn, the highest point en route, Kidsty Pike (780 metres), lies between Patterdale and Shap. Shortly after Shap, you'll cross the M6, marking your departure from the Lake District. A flatter, easier section meanders along the bucolic Eden Valley to Kirkby Stephen where you'll climb to the mysterious Nine Standards Rigg – every year, on 1 January, tenacious (often hungover) fellracers run up to these hilltop cairns. The route across the top, into the Yorkshire Dales, is usually boggy.

◀ DESCENDING GREY KNOTTS TOWARDS HONISTER HAUSE IN THE LAKE DISTRICT.
© STEPHEN ROSS

You'll meet and briefly join the Pennine Way at Keld. Through Swaledale, you can either follow the postcard-perfect river or take a higher route past deserted lead mines across the moorland tops. Many walkers have refreshed themselves at Reeth's Buck Inn – if only because Marske no longer has a pub. Local landowners had the Dormouse Inn's licence revoked after a riotous bonfire night celebration in 1900 saw gates, fences and almost anything else wooden burnt in a massive conflagration.

At Richmond, the largest town on the route, and home to a fine clifftop castle, you leave the Dales behind. Nearly forty kilometres of flat farmland separates you from the next national park, the North York Moors, a section only enlivened by the perilous crossing of the very busy four lanes of the A19. Near the fourteenth-century Mount Grace Priory, the route joins the Cleveland Way National Trail, passing through woodland to reach high moorland. The undulating route over the Cleveland Hills offers stunning views seawards, and across the moors. Near Urra Moor, you'll ascend past the stone buttresses of the Wainstones, with their Bronze Age cup and ring carvings.

At Bloworth Crossing, coast-to-coasters leave the Cleveland Way to follow the trackbed of the old Rosedale Railway. Many a walker has been relieved to see the remote sixteenth-century Lion Inn, looming out of the heathered moorland. Hearty pub suppers and full English breakfasts are staple fare on the Coast to Coast, and you'll be reminded of your overindulgence as you pass Great Fryup Dale (named not for breakfast, but for the Norse goddess Freya, a hint that you are firmly in Viking territory here). At Grosmont, you'll encounter another historic railway line, but steam trains still puff up and down the picturesque North Yorkshire Moors Railway to Whitby.

After a pretty woodland section, past a waterfall at Littlebeck, you near the coast. You can either proceed through the caravan park to take the clifftop route, or follow the Cinder Track along the old Scarborough to Whitby train line. Robin Hood's Bay, once a haven for smugglers, hides itself in a fissure in the cliffs, and a steep road threads down between homely guesthouses to the

Bay Hotel, where you can walk down the slipway to dip your feet in the North Sea and complete your journey.

The Coast to Coast is not always waymarked and you'll need good navigational skills to complete the route, particularly as it is often swathed in fog, even in the summer. You should also expect to encounter rain, particularly on the verdant slopes of the Lake District. Only the hardiest of walkers would attempt the Coast to Coast between October and March, and they may find themselves challenged by the lack of accommodation and other facilities at that time of year, as well as the weather and short days.

Many walkers choose to camp – this approach needs careful planning as, particularly in the Lake District, there are limited opportunities to replenish food and other supplies. As one of the most popular UK trails, walkers are well catered for with respect to bed and breakfast accommodation. There are also plenty of hostels and bunkhouses on the route, although you would be well-advised to book your accommodation far in advance, particularly in the summer months. St Bees is on the Cumbrian Coast line, which connects to the West Coast Main Line at Carlisle. Robin Hood's Bay is no longer served by trains, but buses run along the coast, connecting with railway stations at Whitby and Scarborough.

One man's vision of the perfect walk has inspired tens of thousands to cross an entire country from coast to coast. When the sun breaks through the clouds, England has no finer views to offer than over the sparkling waters of the Lake District or across the purple heathered Cleveland Hills down to the Yorkshire Coast. And when you have admired the fine sunsets and star-studded canopy of England's darkest skies, you're sure to find fellow walkers to share a pint with in a village pub, not much changed since Wainwright first walked the route.

KIDSTY PIKE, ABOVE HAWESWATER. © STEPHEN ROSS

REACHING TRAIL'S END AT ROBIN HOOD'S BAY. © ADAM LONG

TRAIL ESSENTIALS

Start:	**St Bees, Cumbria, England**
End:	**Robin Hood's Bay, North Yorkshire, England**
Distance:	**281km**
Ascent/descent:	**6,020m/6,030m**

HOW TO GET THERE

St Bees has rail connections to Carlisle – the closest international airports are Manchester, Glasgow or Edinburgh.

Robin Hood's Bay is served by the coastal bus service between Whitby and Scarborough – rail connections can be made at either Whitby or Scarborough. The closest international airports are Leeds Bradford Airport and Doncaster Sheffield Airport.

TIME TO COMPLETE

Walking:	**14 days/84 hours**
Trekking:	**9 days/68 hours**
Fastpacking:	**6 days/51 hours**
Trail running:	**5 days/37 hours**

PROS

- **Your own path** – this is not a route that mandates your path or your schedule. All that is defined is the start and finish. You can choose the mountains, or the valleys. You can seek shelter from bad weather or revel in the blustery ridges. The Coast to Coast is about finding your own path.

- **Three national parks** – the Coast to Coast traverses the Lake District, the Yorkshire Dales and the North York Moors.

- **YHA** – there are independent hostels and characterful bunkhouses en route, but the Coast to Coast showcases the best of England's Youth Hostel Association. In the Lake District, you can enjoy the remote Black Sail and the peaceful, recently refurbished Patterdale. Near journey's end, you can enjoy Boggle Hole at the back of the beach, in the cliff's cleft.

CONS

- **A19 road crossing** – the notorious four lanes of the A19 make few concessions to walkers – cars hurtle along this road at more than sixty miles (100 kilometres) per hour.

- **Navigation** – it is not simply that there is no official route and unreliable waymarking. It is that there are helpful signposts that suddenly stop in the wilds.

GOOD TO KNOW

Mike Hartley holds the fastest known time for completing the Coast to Coast. He completed the route in thirty-nine hours and thirty-six minutes in 1991, one of many long-distance records he broke in the 1980s and 1990s – Mike set new fastest times for the Dales Way, the Southern Upland Way and the Pennine Way.

FURTHER INFORMATION

Wainwright's original guidebook, *A Coast to Coast Walk*, is still in print (in an updated version); *The Coast to Coast Walk* (Cicerone, 2017); Harvey maps of the route are also available.

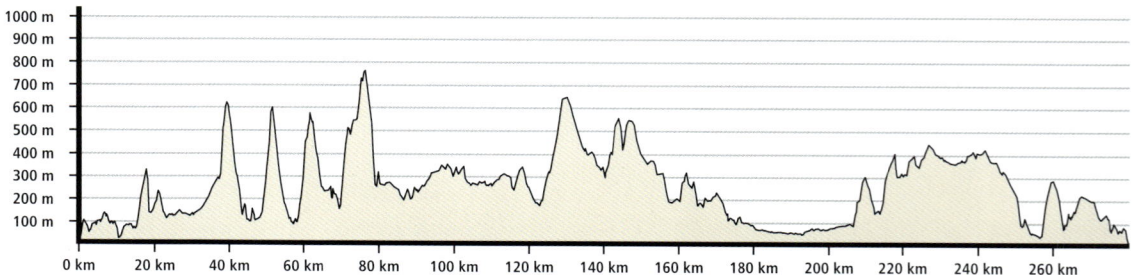

JAN	FEB	MAR	APR	MAY	JUN	JUL	AUG	SEP	OCT	NOV	DEC

SCOTLAND
ENGLAND
Dumfries
A68
Newcastle upon Tyne
Sunderland
North Sea
Carlisle
Alston
M6
Durham
Maryport
North Pennines AONB
Penrith
Keswick
A592
The Pennines
Stockton-on-Tees
Whitehaven
Ennerdale Bridge
High Stile
Rosthwaite
Helvellyn
Ullswater
Patterdale
Rosgill
Shap
River Eden
Barnard Castle
A1(M)
Darlington
Middlesbrough
Whitby
St Bees
Egremont
Great Gable
Scafell Pike
Lake District National Park
Grasmere
Kidsty Pike
Keld
Orton
Kirkby Stephen
Keld
Reeth
Richmond
A19
Grosmont
Robin Hood's Bay
Windermere
Catterick
Osmotherley
Blowoth Crossing
Northallerton
North York Moors National Park
Windermere
Sedbergh
Kendal
A684
Yorkshire Dales National Park
Irish Sea
Grange-over-Sands
Scarborough
Millom
Barrow-in-Furness
Ripon
A1(M)
M6
Lancaster
Skipton
Harrogate
York
N
Forest of Bowland AONB
Blackpool
M55
M65
0
20 Kilometres
Preston
Burnley
Bradford
Leeds
Hull
Blackburn
Wakefield

24 WEST HIGHLAND WAY – 153km

The 153-kilometre West Highland Way leads you out of Scotland's friendliest city, past lochs and forests, to walk across wild moors in the shadows of Munros. While the Devil's Staircase is not as forbidding as it sounds, there are still hills to be conquered, rivers to be forded and midges to be dreaded. A popular choice with the novice long-distance walker, because of its easy navigation and relatively low route, its challenges are often underestimated. Its rewards, however, are panoramic views on a route that takes you past Scotland's largest loch and Britain's highest mountain.

The route, like several of Britain's long-distance trails, has an inauspicious start in the suburban outskirts of a large city. This should serve to remind you that, however urban the area, you're never that far from the best of the British countryside. Just outside Milngavie, you'll pass through Mugdock Wood, a country park donated to the citizens of Glasgow by Sir Hugh Fraser, department store magnate, in 1981. The route begins gently, along pleasant woodland and river trails. At Craigallian Loch, you get your first glimpses of the wilder country in front of you. Near Dumgoyach, you'll pass beneath the standing stones, which are worth a short detour, although you might prefer to leave the route to visit the Glengoyne Distillery. Glengoyne is unique, in that its stills are in the Highlands but, separated by just a road, the whisky matures in sherry casks in the Lowlands.

Leaving the village of Drymen, you'll catch your first view of Loch Lomond, but don't get too excited – the loch is more than thirty-five kilometres long and the route will lead you on a less direct route right along eastern shores to the northernmost tip of the lake. Many walkers spend the best part of two days on the loch's shore and breathe a sigh of relief when they finally conquer it.

The first challenging climb is the ascent to circumvent the summit of Conic Hill, 'the hill above the bog'; you can climb to the very top, at 361 metres, if you relish the extra challenge. Beneath you, you'll see the loch, dotted with islands. Loch Lomond has more than thirty islands, some inhabited. One, Inchconnachan, is populated with wallabies thanks to Lady Fiona of Arran, although despite the popular local myths, there's little evidence that the marsupials have escaped across the loch's frozen waters to take up residence on the mainland. Not unusually on the West Highland Way, the knee-jarring descent down to the loch is perhaps more challenging than the ascent.

Another steep climb up Craigie Fort is your introduction to the tough section around the loch. The Way takes you on dark, mossy forest paths with tree roots to stumble over and streams to ford. At Rowardennan, a picturesque youth hostel nestles on the shores with spectacular views over the water and up Ben Lomond, Scotland's most southerly Munro.

◄ THE WEST HIGHLAND WAY CLIMBS UP CONIC HILL.
© SHUTTERSTOCK/JURIAN CUYPERS

THE DEVIL'S STAIRCASE, GLEN COE. © ALEX RODDIE

At Inversnaid, there's a garrison, built to try and impose English control over Clan MacGregor, a reminder that this is some of the most fiercely fought over territory in Scotland. The West Highland Way often follows the Military Roads built under the command of General Wade to allow the government to deploy troops rapidly if faced with Jacobite uprisings. Many walkers choose to make a brief scramble off-route to see the outlaw Rob Roy's cave.

Towards the end of the loch, you'll see the picturesque ruins of a sixteenth-century castle on Island I Vow. The southern end of the loch was gently rolling countryside but by the time you reach the northern tip, you are confronted with mountains, often snow-topped. At Ardleish, you leave the loch and a short climb lets you look back along the length of the loch and marvel at your achievement.

Most walkers will pause at the quirky Drovers Inn at Inverarnan for a refreshing drink. The West Highland Way has sometimes been described as a long-distance pub crawl and, with 30,000 people walking it every year (and twice as many again walking shorter sections), it is one of the more social long-distance trails. You will probably find yourself meeting the same co-ramblers evening after evening.

The Falls of Falloch, tumbling down from glen, are one of the more spectacular of the many waterfalls passed en route. As you follow the A82 and the West Highland Railway, the forest that you walk through is under the shadows of the Munros: Ben More, Ben Challum, Beinn Dubhchraid, Ben Lui. If you look skywards, you might see buzzards and eagles.

At the Bridge of Orchy, you leave the railway and head towards the wildest and most beautiful section of the route. The path across Rannoch Moor is a drovers' route across ten kilometres of bleak, black peated moor with a constant backdrop of mountains. The Kingshouse Hotel, one of many inns claiming to be Scotland's oldest, sits near to Buachaille Etive Mor, the gateway to Glen Coe. The pub was used after the Battle of Culloden as barracks for the King's troops; today you are more likely to see the neighbouring herd of red deer.

The steady climb up the Devil's Staircase leads you to the saddle between Stob Mhic Mhartuin and Beinn Bheag,

LOCH LOMOND FROM CONIC HILL. © ALEX RODDIE

the highest point on the route at approximately 550 metres. It is a treacherously difficult descent to Kinlochleven, treachery being the order of the day here as it was at Kinlochleven that the Massacre of Glencoe began. In February 1692 troops swept up Glen Coe, killing the members of Clan MacDonald and burning their homes, an injustice particularly sorely felt as the troops had been quartered with the MacDonalds, relying on their hospitality, until the massacre began.

The Glen Nevis Youth Hostel sits under the shadow of Ben Nevis and many choose to end their West Highland Way with a climb to the summit of the mountain, although the route officially ends at the Sore Feet statue in Fort William's Gordon Square.

Fort William is a popular tourist destination, and has both coach and rail connections to Glasgow. Glasgow has an international airport, and good rail connections to other UK cities. However, the West Highland Way is not well served by public transport, although it occasionally corresponds with the West Highland Railway, and its frequent proximity to the A82 does provide opportunity for pickups.

There is a variety of accommodation available along the route with several youth hostels, bed and breakfasts, inns and hotels. However, the route is extremely popular and, particularly in summer, it is best to plan ahead and reserve accommodation well in advance. Wild camping is legal across Scotland, although camping along some of the shores of Loch Lomond is restricted from March to September.

Scotland's dreaded midges are worst in the summer months, and winter's weather may be extremely challenging. Spring and autumn are probably the best seasons to attempt the Way. While the route is waymarked and clear, and has few exposed sections, you will often find yourself far from the nearest village and the settlements that you do reach often have limited amenities.

Many who walk the West Highland Way return to walk it again and again, perhaps to experience the glorious solitude of Rannoch Moor. You'll find companionship along the way, in the trials and adventures of your fellow hikers but, if you're fortunate enough, you may also encounter red deer, otters, kittiwakes or even wildcats.

TRAIL ESSENTIALS

Start:	**Milngavie, Scotland**
End:	**Fort William, Scotland**
Distance:	**153km**
Ascent/descent:	**2,950m/3,010m**

HOW TO GET THERE

Milngavie has frequent rail (and bus) services to Glasgow stations, which connect to other Scottish and English cities. Glasgow has an international airport.

Fort William is nearly four hours by train from Glasgow (the closest international airport). The Caledonian Sleeper offers an overnight, direct rail connection from Fort William to London (Euston).

TIME TO COMPLETE

Walking:	**8 days/45 hours**
Trekking:	**5 days/37 hours**
Fastpacking:	**4 days/28 hours**
Trail running:	**3 days/20 hours**

PROS

• **Highland views** – the West Highland Way offers easy access to spectacular views, showing off the best of the mountains without requiring you to climb them. The rugged mountains rising high above the green Glen Coe are one of Scotland's finest views, but the route offers other delights such as the remote Rannoch Moor, a peaty haven for wildlife.

• **Loch Lomond** – this iconic loch is the largest lake (by surface area) in Great Britain, and marks the boundary between Lowlands and Highlands. The Way besides the loch offers panoramic views of the Highlands in front of you, and Rowardennan Lodge Youth Hostel on the shores of the loch offers stunning lakeside views.

• **Pubs** – many West Highland Wayers choose to relax with a hearty pub meal and a pint of heavy, or a dram of whisky. By Loch Lomond, you may encounter a ghost in the 300-year-old Drovers Inn. The Kingshouse Hotel, rising out of the bogs between Rannoch Moor and Glen Coe, is possibly Scotland's oldest licensed premises and always a welcome sight to weary walkers. In the Boots Bar of the Clachaig Inn, you can eavesdrop on the mountain climbers.

CONS

• **Insects** – in summer, you will be tormented by Scotland's infamous midges, and horse-flies. Ticks, which may carry Lyme disease, are on the increase in the Scottish Highlands.

• **Weather** – even the sunniest days can quickly turn to rain, and fine views will often be obscured by mist or rain. Heavy rain can cause burns to rise rapidly (although most now have bridge crossings). In the winter, snow can be a hazard and, in the worst weather, it is sensible to carry an ice axe.

• **Popularity** – in excess of 30,000 people attempt the West Highland Way each year – the trail will be busy in summer months, and you should book accommodation several months in advance.

GOOD TO KNOW

Every year, runners in the West Highland Way Race, one of the world's oldest ultra marathons, attempt to run the West Highland Way in less than thirty-five hours – every finisher is presented with a glass goblet. Rob Sinclair (thirteen hours and forty-one minutes) and Lucy Colquhoun (seventeen hours and sixteen minutes) hold the course records.

FURTHER INFORMATION

www.westhighlandway.org
West Highland Way Guidemap (Vertebrate Publishing, 2020)

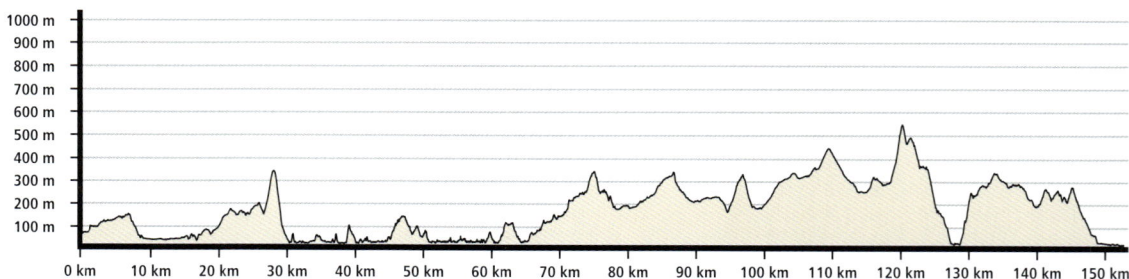

JAN	FEB	MAR	APR	MAY	JUN	JUL	AUG	SEP	OCT	NOV	DEC

Fort William

Glen Nevis

A82

North Ballachulish

Glencoe

Glenachulish

Barcaldine

B845

Ben Cruachan

Dalmally

Inveraray

A819

Cairndow

A815

Garelochhead

Helensburgh

Balloch

Alexandria

Dunoon

Gourock

Greenock

Dumbarton

Erskine

M8

Stob Choire Claurigh

Ben Nevis

Sgor an Iubhair

Binnein Mor

Loch Eilde Mor

Kinlochleven

Devil's Staircase

Glen Coe

A82

Stob Coire nam Beith

Glencoe National Nature Reserve

Clach Leathad

Stob Ghabhar

Inveroran

Bridge of Orchy

A82

Beinn Udlaidh

Tyndrum

Beinn Chuirn

Ben Oss

Inverarnan

Ardlui

Tarbet

Tullich Hill

A814

A82

Loch Lomond

Rowardennan

Ben Lomond

Inversnaid

Conic Hill

Balmaha

Loch Lomond

Drymen

Killearn

A809

Milngavie

Glasgow

Kirkintilloch

M80

Lennoxtown

A811

Callander

Locnearnhead

Loch Earn

Loch Tay

Meall Garbh

Meall Ghaordaidh

Loch Lyon

Cam Chreag

Meall Bhuidhe

A85

Crianlarich

Stob Binnein

Beinn Chabhair

Loch Katrine

Loch Lomond and The Trossachs National Park

A81

Auchtertyre

Creag Mhòr

Beinn Achaladair

Loch Tulla

Rannoch Moor

SCOTLAND

Kingshouse

Blackwater Reservoir

Leum Uilleim

Loch Treig

Geal-Chàrn

Ben Alder

Loch Ericht

Loch Rannoch

Kinloch Rannoch

N

0   10 Kilometres

DUBLIN

25 WICKLOW WAY
– 128km

Dublin is one of Europe's most exciting capital cities – a bustling, friendly maze of historic streets, a city that feels both rooted in the past and fresh-faced. But not far from the cities, Ireland is still a country of tiny rural villages that seem a long way from each other; farming communities where traditional ways of life have not quite been abandoned. The 128-kilometre Wicklow Way leads you from Dublin to the emerald heart of Ireland, across mountains and through forests and farms. As you traverse County Wicklow, you will find yourself a long way from the city, sometimes a long way from anybody. The Wicklow Way was Ireland's first hiking trail, created by J.B. Malone, who had a vision of a network of trails across the country.

The Wicklow Way starts just outside Dublin, next to Marlay House, which was built by the first governor of the Bank of Ireland in 1764. Now owned by the local council, the surrounding grounds are a popular recreational park and also host large concerts – Green Day, Radiohead and R.E.M have all performed here. Marlay Park is home to the Longitude Festival in early July – perhaps not a good time to start the Wicklow Way.

After walking through the park, and crossing under the M50 motorway, you'll be faced with the first climbs en route. The route contours around Two Rock Mountain, on top of which there is a Bronze Age cairn known as Fairy Castle. You'll get your first glimpses of the Wicklow Mountains in front of you. As the route passes over Prince William's Seat, you'll cross from County Dublin into County Wicklow.

At Knockree, there is a youth hostel en route – as the Way was designed to avoid towns and villages, you will often have to divert two or three kilometres off the route for accommodation, food and other facilities. After a climb past the pretty Powerscourt Waterfall, Ireland's highest waterfall at 121 metres, you'll contour around Djouce, although you might choose to make the short detour to its 725-metre summit. The Way passes close to the site where, in August 1946, a plane, carrying twenty-one French Girl Guides visiting their Irish counterparts, crashed. All passengers survived, after a twelve-hour wait on the exposed mountainside, after the leaders and pilot managed to reach the Glencree Valley to raise the alarm.

If you don't summit Djouce, the summit of White Hill (630 metres) is the highest point on the Wicklow Way. As you emerge from Ballinastoe Wood, on to the Barr, you'll reach the J.B. Malone memorial stone where you can pause to enjoy the views down towards Lough Tay. The sand-topped long lake is nicknamed the Guinness Lake, because it looks like a pint – it is fittingly owned by the Guinness family who imported the sand on the shore. On a boreen near Oldbridge, you pass the Wart Stone – the bullaun or bowl stone there is said to cure warts. You'll follow the mass path, once leading the faithful to church, to pine-shaded Brockagh Forest and then on to Glendalough, with its monastic settlement, the remains of a sixth-century site founded by St Kevin. There are very few facilities en route, so you may choose to divert one kilometre off the trail to the pretty village of Laragh, where you'll find shops, bars and occasionally on Sunday a country market.

◄ LOOKING ACROSS THE NORTH WICKLOW HILLS FROM RAVENS ROCK.
© WWW.ADRIANHENDROFF.COM

As you walk up out of the Glendalough Valley, you'll pass the Poulanass Waterfall that separates the valley's two lakes. As you reach the shoulder between Mullacor and Lugduff, you'll be able to see Lugnaquilla, the highest of the Wicklow Mountains. Descending into Glenmalure, the longest glacier valley in Ireland, you'll join the Military Road – the old Military Road runs north to south down the spine of the Wicklow Mountains and was built in the 1800s after the 1798 Rebellion, when rebel troops took advantage of the inaccessibility of the Wicklow Mountains to hide.

The route from Glenmalure again takes advantage of the Military Road, and forestry tracks. At Drumgoff – the halfway point of the Wicklow Way – you can see the remains of the military barracks built for the soldiers of the Military Road. Although the Way is now leaving the higher slopes behind it, and moving into a more gentle forest and farmland section, you'll be rewarded with glimpses of

wildlife. The forests are home to deer and hares, native woodlands to peregrine falcons and red squirrels, and in the Avonbeg River you may glimpse an otter or two.

Although you have left the mountains, you will still struggle to find food or accommodation directly en route, although you will pass one of only four pubs directly on the Way. Tallon's at Stranakelly is now better known as the Dying Cow, because a wily landlady told the Gardai (police) that she was not serving out of hours, but refreshing kindly neighbours who were helping with her dying cow. The pub is believed to date from the mid-eighteenth century. The other pubs on the Way are the Glendalough Hotel, the Glenmalure Lodge and Osborne's in Clonegal.

Osborne's is where walkers traditionally finish the Way. Before enjoying a pint at the coffin-lid bar and claiming your certificate of completion, you must follow a circuitous

THE WICKLOW WAY, SIGNED BY THE YELLOW MAN, ABOVE CURTLESTOWN WOODS. © WWW.ADRIANHENDROFF.COM

route along the tracks of the Raheenakit Forest and then follow the River Derry towards Clonegal. There is one final road section to be endured into the village. Clonegal, nicknamed 'the Switzerland of Ireland' for its beauty, sits between the Wicklow Mountains and the Blackstairs Mountains. You can visit, and even stay at, the ivy-covered Huntington Castle, although there are rumours that the ghosts of druids haunt the seventeenth-century towers.

The route is generally on roads, trails and good paths; the southern half is largely on roads and forestry tracks. Where it passes over bog, sections are often boarded to protect the fragile habitat. The Way tends to the shoulders of mountains, rather than their summits, largely to avoid erosion. The Wicklow Way is one end of the Irish Coast-to-Coast trail – at the other end of the route, which is actually five connected trails, is the Kerry Way. Although the Way is usually walked north to south, walking south to north might be preferable – the southern section features longer road sections, and tracks through conifer forests; a gentle introduction to the route which enables you to enjoy the higher hills and sweeping views on the last days. And what better destination than Dublin to celebrate your achievement. Whichever direction you choose, you'll enjoy pretty waterfalls, high mountain views across the loughs and flower-dappled hedgerows. The Wicklow Way is a reminder that even on grey city streets, you are never far from Ireland's green beauty.

THE GLENMACNESS RIVER SEEN FROM THE FOOTBRIDGE ALONG THE WICKLOW WAY NORTH OF LARAGH. © WWW.ADRIANHENDROFF.COM

25 WICKLOW WAY: ESSENTIAL INFORMATION

TRAIL ESSENTIALS

Start:	**Marlay Park, Dublin, Ireland**
End:	**Clonegal, County Carlow, Ireland**
Distance:	**128km**
Ascent/descent:	**3,760m/3,790m**

HOW TO GET THERE

Marlay Park is approximately nine kilometres from Dublin city centre, and is served by direct buses. Dublin has an international airport, rail connections to other cities in Ireland and Northern Ireland, and ferries to Liverpool and Holyhead (in Wales).

Clonegal is not on a bus or rail route – a bus, from Dublin, serves Kildavin (three kilometres from Clonegal) and the larger town of Bunclody (five kilometres). Some choose to connect to the trail at Glendalough or Glenmalure instead – popular tourist destinations with good bus connections to Dublin.

TIME TO COMPLETE

Walking:	**7 days/43 hours**
Trekking:	**5 days/35 hours**
Fastpacking:	**4 days/26 hours**
Trail running:	**3 days/19 hours**

PROS

• **Waterfalls** – in addition to Ireland's highest waterfall, Powerscourt, the Way offers spectacular views of the pretty waterfalls at Glenmacnass and Poulanass.

• **Wicklow Mountains** – many would claim that peat-covered granite Wicklow Mountains offer some of Ireland's finest and wildest walking. The long glacial Valley of Two Lakes, near Glendalough, is one particular highlight of the Wicklow Mountains National Park.

• **Dublin** – this small city is rammed with adventure. Whether you want to explore its literary culture, enjoy the freshest Irish food or make friends at a traditional pub, you'll find it difficult to drag yourself away from the city and start the trail.

CONS

• **Rain** – Ireland's weather is changeable, but you should anticipate rain, even in the summer. The Wicklow Mountains are rarely snowbound but it may rain ten or more days in every month.

• **Conifers** – the southern section, in particular, passes through extensive swathes of modern conifer plantations along forestry tracks.

• **Roads** – Ireland does not enjoy an extensive network of traditional rights of way and, despite J.B. Malone's efforts in negotiating the Wicklow Way, you will often find yourself following a country lane into villages.

GOOD TO KNOW

The Wicklow Mountains are a popular running destination – in addition to the Way, the Wicklow Round is a 100-kilometre challenge route that takes in twenty-six mountain peaks, including the 925-metre-high Lugnaquilla. It must be run in less than twenty-four hours, and was first completed in July 2008 by Moire O'Sullivan.

FURTHER INFORMATION

www.sportireland.ie/outdoors/walking/trails/wicklow-way

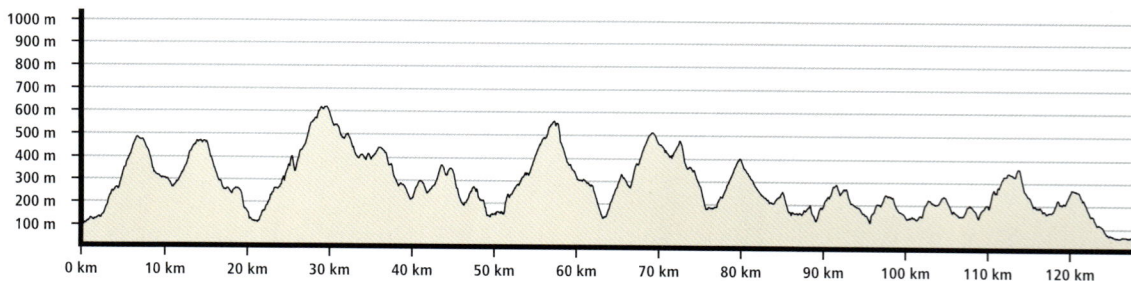

JAN	FEB	MAR	APR	MAY	JUN	JUL	AUG	SEP	OCT	NOV	DEC

Celbridge

Clondalkin

Dublin

Dún Laoghaire

Newcastle

Tallaght

M50

Clane

Marlay Park (S)

Dundrum

Glencullen

Sallins

Brittas

Curtlestown

Bray

Naas

N7

Kippure

River Glencree

R. Dargle

Greystones

Blessington

Poulaphouca Reservoir

Wicklow Mountains

Djouce

White Hill

N11

wbridge

M7

Ballymore Eustace

Mullaghcleevaun

Lough Tay

Sleamaine

R755

Vartry Reservoir Upper

Kilcullen

M9

Valleymount

Wicklow Mountains National Park

Lough Dan

Roundwood

Vartry Reservoir Lower

Hollywood

Dunlavin

N81

Tonelagee

River Glenmacnass

Oldbridge

R412

IRELAND

Conavalla

Upper Lake

Glendalough

Laragh

R755

Camenabologue

River Avonbeg

Wicklow

Baltinglass

Lugnaquilla

Keadeen Mtn

Glenmalure

Rathdrum

M11

Croaghanmoira

Rosahane Bridge

R753

stledermot

Knockananna

Askanagap

River Ow

Aughrim

Arklow

Cross Bridge

Garryhoe

Tullow

Mullinacuft

Tinahely

M11

River Derry

Ballon

Shillelagh

River Slaney

Carnew

River Derry

Gorey

R724

Clonegal (F)

R746

R725

Bunclody

N

0   10 Kilometres

BIG TRAILS
BIG TRAILS
HEART OF EUROPE
THE BEST LONG-DISTANCE TRAILS IN WESTERN EUROPE AND THE ALPS

BIG TRAILS

KATHY ROGERS & STEPHEN ROSS

BIG TRAILS
HEART OF EUROPE

Featuring twenty-five inspirational long-distance trails in Western Europe and the Alps:

01 ... Adlerweg
02 ... Alta Via 1
03 ... Altmühltal-Panoramaweg
04 ... Brabantse Heuvelroute
05 ... Carnic Peace Trail
06 ... Heidschnuckenweg
07 ... Holland's Coast Path
08 ... King Ludwig's Way
09 ... Malerweg
10 ... Meraner Höhenweg
11 ... Mullerthal Trail
12 ... Normandy's Alabaster Coast
13 ... Pfälzer Weinsteig
14 ... Pieterpad
15 ... Rhine Castles Trail
16 ... Salzburger Almenweg
17 ... Stelling van Amsterdam
18 ... Tour de Paris
19 ... Tour du Matterhorn
20 ... Tour du Mont Blanc
21 ... Tour of Monte Rosa
22 ... Traversée du Massif des Vosges
23 ... Walker's Haute Route: Chamonix to Zerma
24 ... Walserweg
25 ... Westweg

ALPKIT

NICE PLACES GO DO GOOD THINGS SINCE '04

Start your adventure at *alpkit.com* or visit an Alpkit store.

Technical outdoor gear that costs less and works harder.

#goniceplacesdogoodthings
#sonderstories

**RUN HIKE
CLIMB CAMP
SWIM BIKE**

BIG TRAILS – AT A GLANCE

Trail	PAGE	COUNTRIES	DISTANCE	ASCENT/DESCENT	WALKING TIME (DAYS/HOURS)	TREKKING TIME (DAYS/HOURS)	FASTPACKING TIME (DAYS/HOURS)	TRAIL RUNNING TIME (DAYS/HOURS)
01 A Dales High Way	3	England	143km	3,770m/3,690m	8/46	5/37	4/28	3/20
02 Beara Way	9	Ireland	211km	5,850m/5,740m	12/69	7/56	5/42	4/30
03 Cambrian Way	15	Wales	462km	17,540m/17,540m	29/173	18/139	13/105	9/73
04 Cape Wrath Trail	21	Scotland	378km	11,010m/10,900m	21/126	13/102	10/77	7/54
05 Causeway Coast Way	27	Northern Ireland	53km	740m/760m	3/14	2/12	2/9	1/7
06 Cleveland Way	33	England	174km	3,600m/3,630m	9/51	6/42	4/32	3/23
07 Cotswold Way	39	England	168km	3,750m/3,860m	9/51	5/41	4/31	3/22
08 Dales Way	45	England	127km	1,507m/1,600m	6/33	4/27	3/20	2/15
09 Hadrian's Wall Path	51	England	138km	1,330m/1,340m	6/35	4/28	3/21	2/16
10 Icknield Way Path	57	England	182km	1,560m/1,760m	7/44	5/36	4/27	3/21
11 Isle of Anglesey Coastal Path	63	Wales	201km	2,190m/2,190m	8/50	5/41	4/31	3/23
12 John Muir Way	69	Scotland	213km	1,830m/1,810m	9/51	6/42	4/32	3/24
13 Kerry Way	75	Ireland	202km	4,700m/4,700m	10/62	6/50	5/38	4/27
14 London LOOP	81	England	230km	1,840m/1,840m	9/55	6/45	5/34	4/26
15 Offa's Dyke Path	87	Wales, England	287km	7,650m/7,660m	15/92	9/75	7/56	5/40
16 Peddars Way and Norfolk Coast Path	93	England	214km	1,040m/1,060m	8/48	5/39	4/30	3/23
17 Pennine Way	99	England, Scotland	411km	9,870m/10,010m	21/128	13/104	10/78	7/56
18 Raad ny Foillan	105	Isle of Man	157km	2,840m/2,840m	7/44	5/36	4/27	3/20
19 South Downs Way	111	England	162km	3,230m/3,240m	8/47	5/39	4/29	3/21
20 South West Coast Path	117	England	986km	18,230m/18,260m	47/281	29/230	22/172	16/126
21 Thames Path	123	England	294km	1,010m/1,120m	11/64	7/53	5/40	4/31
22 The Ridgeway	129	England	140km	1,870m/1,790m	6/36	4/30	3/23	3/17
23 Wainwright's Coast to Coast	135	England	281km	6,020m/6,030m	14/84	9/68	6/51	5/37
24 West Highland Way	141	Scotland	153km	2,950m/3,010m	8/45	5/37	4/28	3/20
25 Wicklow Way	147	Ireland	128km	3,760m/3,790m	7/43	5/35	4/26	3/19

The table also includes columns for TRAIL ICONS and a WHEN TO GO grid covering the months J F M A M J J A S O N D.